"Mark Roberts has produced what has long been needed: a highly readable and compelling account of why Christians can indeed trust the Gospels. Dr. Roberts is a formidable scholar whose reputation is very high among academics. He is a skilled writer and teacher. He is also an innovative force in the world of Christian apologetics, among the very first to see the potential for blogging as a formidable means of pursuing the Great Commission.

"I have had Dr. Roberts on my radio show more than any other theologian or pastor, for several reasons. First, he has been a very good friend for a long time. But much more important is his ability to communicate and the knowledge he has accumulated through his three decades of serious and thorough study of the Gospels and the scholarship around them. Whenever a major controversy erupts that touches on the Christian faith, I call on Dr. Roberts.

"*Can We Trust the Gospels?* is quite simply the best effort I have ever read by a serious scholar to communicate what scholars know about the Gospels and why that should indeed encourage us to trust them and thus to trust Jesus Christ."

—Hugh Hewitt, radio talk show host, author, blogger,
and Professor of Law at Chapman University School of Law

"There is a crisis of confidence about the Gospels, fueled by sensational claims about supposedly new Gnostic Gospels with a 'revised standard' view of Jesus. With a pastor's insight but a scholar's critical acumen, Mark Roberts provides a readable guide to answering the question, Can we trust the Gospels? As Mark makes clear, the earliest and best evidence we have for the real Jesus is the canonical Gospels, not the much later Gnostic ones."

—Ben Witherington III, Professor of New Testament,
Asbury Theological Seminary, author of
What Ha

"What F. F. Bruce did for my generation o\[f\]
done for the current generation. Any student
are reliable will be given this book, and then
next student!"

—Scot McKnight, Karl A. Olsson Professor in Religious Studies,
North Park University

"*Can We Trust The Gospels?* caught me completely by surprise. While I knew a scholar of Mark Roberts's caliber could convince skeptics the Gospels are reliable, I never expected to have my own preconceptions uprooted and replaced with a more solid trust in these biblical texts. This book not only makes a compelling case for trusting the Gospels, it illuminates the creative ways in which God worked to bring us His Word. Roberts's brilliant little book deserves to be widely read by both skeptics and believers."

—Joe Carter, blogger (evangelicaloutpost.com) and Director of Communications for the Family Research Council

Can We Trust the Gospels?

Investigating the Reliability of
Matthew, Mark, Luke, and John

Mark D. Roberts

CROSSWAY BOOKS
WHEATON, ILLINOIS

Can We Trust the Gospels? Investigating the Reliability of Matthew, Mark, Luke, and John
Copyright © 2007 by Mark D. Roberts
Published by Crossway Books
a publishing ministry of Good News Publishers
1300 Crescent Street
Wheaton, Illinois 60187

Published in association with Yates and Yates, LLP, Attorneys and Counselors, Orange, California.

Cover design: Josh Dennis
Cover illustration: The Bridgeman Art Library

Photo credits: The four views of Half Dome courtesy of Mark D. Roberts. The synagogue in Capernaum, the Pilate inscription, and the Pool of Siloam courtesy of Holy Land Photos (www. HolyLandPhotos.org). The cliffs at El Kursi courtesy of Kim Guess/BiblePlaces.com. All photos used by permission.

First printing 2007
Printed in the United States of America

ISBN-10: 1-58134-866-5
ISBN-13: 978-1-58134-866-8

Library of Congress Cataloging-in-Publication Data
Roberts, Mark D.
    Can we trust the Gospels? : investigating the reliability of Matthew, Mark, Luke, and John / Mark D. Roberts.
      p. cm.
    Includes bibliographical references and index.
    ISBN 978-1-58134-866-8 (tpb)

     1. Bible. N.T. Gospels—Criticism, interpretation, etc. I. Title.

BS2555.52.R63 2007
226'.06—dc22
                                        2007005924

VP   16   15   14   13   12   11   10   09   08
           10   9   8   7   6   5   4   3   2

This book is dedicated to Don Williams,
with gratitude,
for his example of faithfulness as a scholar-pastor,
for his energetic commitment to the truth,
and for the encouragement he's given me throughout the years

Contents

CONTENTS

Illustrations

Acknowledgments

First, I want to thank those who have helped to make this book a reality. The visionaries at Crossway Books, Geoff Dennis, Lane Dennis, and Al Fisher, saw the potential in my blog series on the Gospels and encouraged me to turn it into a "blook." Bill Deckard, my editor at Crossway, has been a great help along the way. My literary agent, Curtis Yates of Yates and Yates, LLP, was, as always, a valued partner. Ben Witherington III was kind enough to read an early manuscript of the book and offer useful criticisms and suggestions.

I want also to thank my congregation at Irvine Presbyterian Church for their ongoing partnership in ministry. I'm especially grateful to the members of the Pastor's Study for their support and teamwork in the search for God's truth.

Thanks are due to many blog readers who expressed appreciation for my series on the Gospels, as well as to those whose critical comments urged me to sharpen my arguments.

I'm grateful to those who have helped me understand the Gospels through their teachings and writings, including: George MacRae, Harvey Cox, Helmut Koester, Ben Witherington III, N. T. Wright, Craig L. Blomberg, and F. F. Bruce.

Thanks to friends who have cheered me on in the writing of this book: Hugh Hewitt, Tod Bolsinger, Lee Strobel, Tim McCalmont, Bill White, Doug Gregg, and Terry Tigner.

As always, my heartfelt thanks go to my wife, Linda, and my children, Nathan and Kara, for their tireless love and support. They are my best partners in all things.

Chapter 1

A Bio and a Blook

In this book I seek to answer a simple question: *Can we trust the Gospels?*

I'm thinking of two different but related dimensions of trust. On the one hand, I'm asking if the Gospels provide *reliable historical information* about Jesus of Nazareth. On the other hand, I'm wondering if they offer a *trustworthy basis for faith* in Jesus. In this book I will focus almost exclusively on the historical dimension of trusting the Gospels.

When I speak of "the Gospels," I'm referring to the first four books of the Christian New Testament. There are other so-called "Gospels" among extrabiblical collections of ancient writings, most famously in the Nag Hammadi Library of Gnostic writings. Though these documents rarely focus on the life and ministry of the human Jesus, they may occasionally contain tidbits of historical data about him. I'll refer to the noncanonical Gospels when appropriate in this book, but they are not my primary concern.

I should come clean at this point and admit that I do indeed believe that the Gospels are trustworthy. But I have not always been so confident about their reliability. There was a time when I would have answered the "Can we trust the Gospels?" question with, "Well, maybe, at least somewhat. But I have my doubts." How I got to a place of confidence from this earlier point of uncertainty is a story that will help you grasp "where I'm coming from," as we would say in California.

Doubting the Gospels

I grew up in a solid evangelical church. The Gospels were assumed to be not only historically accurate but also inspired by God. In my teenage years I wondered about the trustworthiness of the Gospels. But my youth leaders reassured me. I was encouraged to learn that the inspiration of the Gospels was proved by the similarities between Matthew, Mark, and Luke. Who else, besides the Holy Spirit, could inspire the evangelists[1] to compose such amazingly parallel accounts of Jesus?

I went to college at Harvard. Though founded as a Christian school, and though the university seal continues to proclaim *veritas christo et ecclesiae*, "Truth for Christ and the Church," Harvard in the 1970s wasn't exactly a bastion of Christian faith. Plus, I was planning to major in philosophy, a discipline notorious for its atheistic bias. Many of my friends back home worried that I would lose my faith at "godless Harvard."

During my freshman year, it wasn't my philosophy courses that threw my faith for a loop, however. It was a New Testament class. Religion 140, "Introduction to Early Christian Literature," was taught by Professor George MacRae, a top-notch New Testament scholar. As the semester began, I had my guard up, expecting Professor MacRae to be a Dr. Frankenstein who would create a monster to devour my faith. In fact, however, Professor MacRae was no mad scientist. One of the best lecturers I ever had at Harvard, he seasoned his reasonable pre-

---

1. In biblical studies, "evangelists" refers to the writers of the Gospels. "Gospel" in Greek is *euangelion*. From this we get the word "evangelist," meaning "preacher of good news."

sentations with humorous quips among hundreds of valuable insights. His first lecture on the challenges of studying early Christianity was so impressive to me that I still remember his main points and use them when I teach seminary courses on the New Testament.

Professor MacRae followed this lecture with a fascinating exploration of the world of early Christianity. Next he turned to the letters of Paul. Though he investigated them as a critical scholar,[2] his insights fit more or less with what I had learned in church. My guard began to come down.

But then we came to the Gospels. Professor MacRae did not deny their usefulness as historical sources. But he did argue that these documents, though containing some historical remembrances, were chock-full of legendary elements, including miracle stories, exorcisms, and prophecies. These were not to be taken as part of the historical record, he said. Rather, they were best understood as fictional elements added by the early Christians to increase the attractiveness of Jesus in the Greco-Roman world. The Gospels were not so much historical or biographical documents as they were theological tractates weaving together powerful fictions with a few factual data.

Perhaps what most shook my faith in the trustworthiness of the Gospels was Professor MacRae's treatment of the similarities among Matthew, Mark, and Luke. He explained persuasively that Mark was the first of the Gospels to be written, and that Matthew and Luke used Mark in their writing. In the process, he also demonstrated how Matthew and Luke changed Mark, interjecting "contradictions" into the Gospel record.

Listening to this explanation of why the Synoptic[3] Gospels were so similar, I felt the rug being pulled out from under my

---

2. Critical scholarship involves historical, literary, linguistic, and sociological analysis of the New Testament. It is not necessarily critical in the sense of being negative. In fact hundreds of critical New Testament scholars also affirm the reliability of the Gospels. But many academics, especially in secular institutions, blend critical scholarship with pessimistic appraisals of the New Testament, and often with their own personal denigration of Christianity in general.

3. "Synoptic" means "capable of being read side by side, or synoptically." Matthew, Mark, and Luke are synoptic because they are so similar in form and content.

confidence in these writings. Where I had once been taught that these similarities were evidence of divine inspiration, I discovered that a straightforward historical explanation provided a simpler account of the data. *How many other things have I been taught about the Gospels that aren't true?* I wondered.

Uncertain about My Uncertainty

After finishing Religion 140, I could not trust the Gospels to provide historically accurate knowledge of Jesus. Yet, as much as I found this skeptical perspective compelling, it didn't fully satisfy me. Ironically, my studies of philosophy contributed to my uncertainty about my Gospel uncertainty. As a "phil concentrator" I was learning to scrutinize the theoretical underpinnings of all beliefs. It seemed only right to subject what I had learned about the New Testament to this sort of investigation. When I did, I began to wonder if my new perspective on the Gospels was too simplistic.

For example, one of the things that bothered me about Professor MacRae's position was how quickly he concluded that there were *contradictions* among the Gospels. In my philosophy classes I was being trained to assume that a document was consistent unless every effort to discern consistency failed. Though the Gospels were not written by one author, it seemed that Professor MacRae had rushed to judgment about the contradictory nature of the Gospels without considering how varying Gospel accounts might have been complementary.

In my undergraduate years I began to think critically, not only about the New Testament but also about the methodologies and presuppositions of New Testament scholarship. Sometimes, I discovered, academic consensus was built on the shifting sand of weak philosophy, peculiar methodology,[4] and

---

4. For example, ever since I first learned about the "criterion of dissimilarity," a scholarly tool for establishing the validity of historical claims about Jesus, it seemed to me that this was obviously and woefully inadequate, even though it was accepted without hesitation by many critical scholars. For a brief critique of the criterion of

atheistic theology. Perhaps other approaches were possible, ones that involved rigorous New Testament scholarship and led to a more positive appraisal of the Gospels' reliability.

A Strange Twist in the Road

My road to confidence in the Gospels took a strange twist during my junior year. I enrolled in a seminar with Professor MacRae called "Christians, Jews, and Gnostics." Among the documents we studied in this course were several Gnostic writings that had just been published in English. Some of these documents, written in Coptic, had been translated by Professor MacRae for *The Nag Hammadi Library in English*.[5] This meant I had the chance to study these Gnostic texts with one of the world's foremost authorities on them. It never dawned on me, by the way, that someday people outside of academia would care about the contents of the Gnostic Gospels.

In "Christians, Jews, and Gnostics" I learned to dig deeply into the meaning of the ancient texts and to ask all sorts of questions about them. Professor MacRae was willing to engage any serious question, including challenges to his own perspectives. During this second class with him I began to see the Gospels as more reliable than I had once thought, in part, as I compared them to the wildly fictional portraits of Jesus in the Gnostic Gospels.

By the end of this seminar, Professor MacRae encouraged me to pursue graduate work in New Testament. His openness to my questions was one of the reasons I decided to remain at Harvard for my doctoral work. Ironically, the one who was most responsible for my loss of confidence in the Gospels became a primary reason for my growing trust in them.[6]

---

dissimilarity, see http://www.markdroberts.com/htmfiles/resources/unmaskingthejesus. htm#sep1405.

5. James M. Robinson, ed., *The Nag Hammadi Library in English* (New York: Harper & Row, 1977).

6. Professor MacRae would have been my dissertation advisor, had it not been for his untimely death in 1985.

Critical New Testament Scholarship: Up Close and Personal

Without exception, my grad school teachers echoed Professor MacRae's conclusions about the historical limitations of the New Testament Gospels. In fact, several faculty members made him look rather conservative. I did learn a great deal from these scholars, however. Their knowledge of the world of early Christianity was encyclopedic, and their ability to interpret ancient texts critically was superlative. Yet I began to see how often their interpretations were saturated by unquestioned philosophical presuppositions. If, for example, a passage from the Gospels included a prophecy of Jesus concerning his death, it was assumed without argument that this had been added later by the church because prophecy didn't fit within the naturalistic worldview of my profs.[7]

The more I spent time with some of the leading New Testament scholars in the world, the more I came to respect their brilliance and, at the same time, to recognize the limitations of their scholarly perspectives. I saw how often conclusions based on unsophisticated assumptions were accepted without question by the reigning scholarly community, and taught uncritically as if they were, well, the Gospel truth.

I also discovered how rarely my professors entertained perspectives by scholars who didn't share their naturalistic worldview. Evangelical scholars[8] were usually ignored simply because they were conservative. This fact was driven home once when I was on winter break in Southern California. I needed to read a few books for one of my courses, so I went to the Fuller Seminary library because it was close to my home. What I found at Fuller stunned me. Fuller students were required to

7. "Naturalism" is the philosophical position that assumes there is nothing beyond nature, or physical existence. A naturalistic worldview makes no room for supernatural events or a supernatural God.

8. Evangelical scholars are those who believe that the Bible is, in some strong sense, God's inspired Word. Some refer to Scripture as inerrant; others prefer the term infallible. Many evangelical scholars are also critical scholars in that they investigate biblical documents with the tools of academia and engage in dialogue with critical scholars across the theological spectrum.

read many of the same books I was assigned, and also books written from an evangelical perspective. Whereas I was getting one party line, Fuller students were challenged to think more broadly and, dare I admit it, more critically. This put an arrogant Harvard student in his place, let me tell you. It also helped me see how much my own education was lopsided. Only once in my entire graduate school experience was I assigned a book by an evangelical scholar.[9]

Critical Scholarship and Confidence in the Gospels

Beginning with my days at Harvard and continuing throughout the last three decades, I have worked away on the question of the trustworthiness of the Gospels. I have come to believe that there are solid reasons for accepting them as reliable both for history and for faith.

You may be surprised to learn that I agree with about three-quarters of what I learned from Professor MacRae in Religion 140. We affirm the same basic facts: the raw data of ancient documents and archeological discoveries. The differences between our views have to do with how we evaluate the data, and here the gap between what Professor MacRae taught and what I believe today is often wide and deep.

You may also be surprised to discover that my arguments in this book are often friendlier to critical scholarship than you might expect. For example, many defenses of the historical reliability of the Gospel of John depend on an early date of composition (pre–A.D. 70). I will not base my own conclusions upon this early date, though I think there are persuasive arguments in its favor.

While reading this book, an evangelical who is well acquainted with New Testament scholarship might periodically

9. Professor Krister Stendahl assigned a commentary on Matthew by Robert H. Gundry (*Matthew: A Commentary on His Literary and Theological Art* [Grand Rapids, Mich.: Eerdmans, 1982]). Ironically, this book was roundly criticized by many evangelicals as buying too much into non-evangelical approaches to the Gospels.

object, "But there are even stronger arguments than the ones you're making." So be it! I'm open to these positions and glad for those who articulate them. But I have chosen to base my case, for the most part, on that which most even-handed critical scholars, including non-evangelicals, would affirm. I've done this for two reasons.

First, I want to encourage the person who is troubled by negative views of the Gospels, perhaps in a college New Testament course or in a popular "Gospels-debunking" book. In a sense, I'm writing for the Mark Roberts who once felt perplexed in Religion 140. To the "old me" and others like him I want to say, "Look, even if you believe most of 'assured results of scholarship' concerning the Gospels, you can still trust them."

Second, I believe this book will have broader impact if I don't fill it with theories that, however plausible, are popular only among conservative scholars. For example, it may well be that the disciples of Jesus had been trained to memorize sayings of their religious mentors, much like later rabbinic students.[10] If this is true, it would greatly increase the likelihood that the sayings of Jesus in the Gospels closely reflect what Jesus himself had once said. But since the jury is still out on the question of whether or not the disciples were trained in technical memorization, I won't base my conclusions upon this possibility.

My basic point in this book is that if you look squarely at the facts as they are widely understood, and if you do not color them with pejorative bias or atheistic presuppositions, then you'll find that it's reasonable to trust the Gospels.

For those not familiar with the Bible, I should explain that there are four Gospels in the New Testament, a collection of twenty-seven early Christian writings. The New Testament is the second part of the Christian Bible, which also contains a collection of thirty-nine Jewish writings which Christians call

---

10. This view is ably defended by Birger Gerhardsson in *The Reliability of the Gospel Tradition* (Peabody, Mass.: Hendrickson, 2001).

the Old Testament. Jews refer to these thirty-nine writings as the Bible or the *Tanakh* (from the Hebrew words for law, prophecy, and writings).

The Gospels of Matthew, Mark, Luke, and John are the first four books of the New Testament, though they are not the earliest of the New Testament writings. They focus on certain aspects of the life and ministry of Jesus of Nazareth, and especially on his death and resurrection. There are other early Christian writings called Gospels, perhaps two or three dozen depending on what counts as a Gospel. For reasons that I'll explain in this book, the extrabiblical Gospels are not as reliable as historical sources for Jesus, though they sometimes describe Jesus' sayings or actions accurately.

The Birth of a "Blook"

This book is a direct result of my engagement with many attempts to undermine confidence in the Gospels. In the last two years I have publicly defended the Gospels against assaults from a *Newsweek* cover story,[11] the Jesus Seminar,[12] the book *Misquoting Jesus*, by Bart Ehrman,[13] the claims made about the *Gospel of Judas* by some scholars,[14] and, most of all, Dan Brown's best-selling novel, *The Da Vinci Code*.[15] My apologetic[16] writings have appeared on my web site, *www.markdroberts.*

11. Mark D. Roberts, *The Birth of Jesus: Hype or History?* http://www.markd roberts.com/htmfiles/resources/jesusbirth.htm.

12. Mark D. Roberts, *Unmasking the Jesus Seminar,* http://www.markdroberts. com/htmfiles/resources/unmaskingthejesus.htm.

13. Mark D. Roberts, *The Bible, the Qur'an, Bart Ehrman, and the Words of God,* http://www.markdroberts.com/htmfiles/resources/biblequran.htm. See Bart D. Ehrman, *Misquoting Jesus: The Story behind Who Changed the Bible and Why* (New York: HarperSanFrancisco, 2005).

14. Mark D. Roberts, *The Gospel of Judas: A Special Report,* http://www.mark-droberts.com/htmfiles/resources/davinciopportunity3.htm#apr906.

15. Mark D. Roberts, *The Da Vinci Opportunity,* http://www.markdroberts. com/htmfiles/resources/davinciopportunity.htm.

16. "Apologetic" writings offer a reasonable defense of some belief. The word "apologetic" comes from the Greek term *apologia*, which means "defense (written or spoken)." It has no connection at all with the concept of "apologizing" for something.

com, and in other online or print media. As I endeavored to fend off attacks upon the Gospels, it occurred to me that I ought to write a short, popular, positive case for trusting these embattled portraits of Jesus. So in the fall of 2005 I wrote an extended blog series entitled *Are the New Testament Gospels Reliable?*[17]

Since the release of that series I have received hundreds of gratifying e-mails from people who have thanked me. Some notes have included questions or points of correction. Of course I've also received correspondence from people who disagree with my positions. These have helped me clarify and refine my arguments.

Perhaps the most surprising positive response to my blog series came from the publishers at Crossway Books. They said they were interested in turning my series into a book. At first I hesitated, realizing that there are other fine books on the reliability of the Gospels. I fondly remember the classic volume by F. F. Bruce, *The New Testament Documents: Are They Reliable?*[18] which helped me survive my collegiate doubts about the Gospels. I also thought of the more detailed and up-to-date book by Craig Blomberg, *The Historical Reliability of the Gospels.*[19] And I knew that a solid defense of the Gospels called *Reinventing Jesus* was soon to be published.[20] Moreover, I have seen how effective Lee Strobel's *The Case for Christ* has been as a popular apologetic introduction to Jesus and the Gospels.[21] But the more I received communication from people who had been helped by my blog series, the more I realized that I could

17. Mark D. Roberts, *Are the New Testament Gospels Reliable?* http://www.markdroberts.com/htmfiles/resources/gospelsreliable.htm.

18. F. F. Bruce, *The New Testament Documents: Are They Reliable?* (Grand Rapids, Mich.: Eerdmans, 1960).

19. Craig L. Blomberg, *The Historical Reliability of the Gospels* (Downers Grove, Ill.: InterVarsity Press, 1987). Blomberg's book is excellent, and I recommend it highly. It is more detailed than this book and is suitable for readers with knowledge of New Testament studies.

20. J. Ed Komoszewski, M. James Sawyer, and Daniel B. Wallace, *Reinventing Jesus: What the Da Vinci Code and Other Novel Speculations Don't Tell You* (Grand Rapids, Mich.: Kregel, 2006).

21. Lee Strobel, *The Case for Christ: A Journalist's Personal Investigation of the Evidence for Jesus* (Grand Rapids, Mich.: Zondervan, 1998).

offer something unique to book readers. The result, *Can We Trust the Gospels?* is an expanded and, I hope, improved version of my original blog series. It is, according to the new lingo, a blook—a *book* based on a *blog*.

Many of the basic facts and arguments in this book can be found elsewhere, though numerous points and illustrations are new. What makes this book distinctive is its availability to nonspecialists, including non-Christian readers. I realize this will be frustrating for a few readers who are familiar with New Testament scholarship and who will want more extensive discussion and documentation. But *Can We Trust the Gospels?* is meant to be a shorter book that can be easily grasped by people who don't have specialized academic knowledge and who don't want to wade through a much longer tome. This volume could easily have been 500 pages with 5,000 footnotes. But then I'd completely miss my intended audience . . . the ordinary person who wonders, *Can I trust the Gospels?*

Though no longer linked electronically to my web site, this "blook" will continue to be supported through online conversation, clarification, and revision. At *www.markdroberts.com* there will be a place for you to log your comments, ask your questions, or listen in on an ongoing conversation. My web site will also allow me to relate *Can We Trust the Gospels?* to new assaults on their historical reliability. No doubt there will be many of these in the years to come.[22]

F.A.Q. Format

Influence of the Internet can also be seen in the basic format of this book. Millions of web sites use a F.A.Q. page—Frequently Asked Questions—to respond to the most common inquiries from visitors. *Can We Trust the Gospels?* is an extended F.A.Q. It is structured by a series of basic questions about the Gospels:

---

22. For example, as I'm editing this manuscript, a television documentary claims that the bones of Jesus have been found, thus invalidating the Gospel accounts of his death and resurrection.

- Can we know what the original Gospel manuscripts really said?
- Did the evangelists know Jesus personally?
- When were the Gospels written?
- What sources did the Gospel writers use?
- Did early Christian oral tradition reliably pass down the truth about Jesus?
- What are the New Testament Gospels?
- What difference does it make that there are four Gospels?
- Are there contradictions in the Gospels?
- If the Gospels are theology, can they be history?
- Do miracles undermine the reliability of the Gospels?
- Do historical sources from the era of the Gospels support their reliability?
- Does archeology support the reliability of the Gospels?
- Did the political agenda of the early church influence the content of the Gospels?
- Why do we have only four Gospels in the Bible?
- Can we trust the Gospels after all?

The pages ahead contain answers that are the result of more than three decades of investigation, involving hundreds of hours of seminary teaching, thousands of hours of thinking, and myriads of pages of reading. For the sake of my intended audience, I have condensed all of this into relatively few pages. You won't find complex arguments with elaborate footnotes in this book, even though many of my conclusions grow out of such complexity and elaboration. If you're looking for more data than I can provide here, I'll try to point you in helpful directions through the footnotes.

My hope is that, as you read this book, you will come to believe that you can trust the biblical Gospels. Even as Luke wrote the third Gospel so that his readers might "know the truth" concerning Jesus (Luke 1:4), so have I written this book.

Chapter 2

Can We Know What the Original Gospel Manuscripts Really Said?

If you open a Bible and look for the Gospels, you'll find them in English translation, neatly collected at the beginning of the New Testament. You'll see book names, chapter and verse numbers, punctuation, and paragraphs. None of these items were present in the original manuscripts of the writings we call Matthew, Mark, Luke, and John. Most manuscripts didn't even have spaces between the words! Aren'tyougladthingshave changed? What you read in your Bible is the result of centuries of preservation, translation, and publication. Thus you might sensibly wonder, *Do the Gospels bear any resemblance to what the original writers actually penned almost 2,000 years ago?*

It is common these days for people to answer no to this question. Critics of Christianity often allege that the Gospels as we know them don't resemble the originals. This criticism appears, for example, on the lips of Sir Leigh Teabing, a fictional historian in Dan Brown's wildly popular novel *The Da Vinci Code*. Teabing "reveals" the true nature of the Bible in this way:

> "The Bible is a product of *man*. . . . Not of God. The Bible did not fall magically from the clouds. Man created it as a historical record of tumultuous times, and it has evolved through countless translations, additions, and revisions. History has never had a definitive version of the book."[1]

There is a measure of truth here. The Bible is indeed a human product, though this in no way requires that it could not also be "of God." For centuries, Christians have affirmed that the Bible was written by human authors who were inspired by God.

It's true that the Bible "did not fall magically from the clouds." It was in fact written by human beings who lived in "tumultuous times." Yet the biblical documents were not created *primarily* as a "historical record" of these times. Though there is plenty of history in Scripture, the biblical writers weren't telling merely a human story. Rather, they focused primarily on the actions of God in history, especially on the story of God's salvation of the world.

Teabing exaggerates in saying that the Bible has "evolved through countless translations." It has indeed been translated into more languages than any other book, by far. At last count, the New Testament has been translated into 1,541 languages.[2] But the Bible has not "evolved through countless translations," as if our English versions stand at the end of a long chain of multilingual transformations. Every modern translation of Scripture is based on manuscripts written in the same languages as those used by the original writers. The Old Testament in English comes directly from Hebrew and Aramaic manuscripts. Our New Testament is translated from Greek manuscripts.

1. Dan Brown, *The Da Vinci Code* (New York: Doubleday, 2003), 231.
2. http://www.wycliffe.org.uk/aboutus_whatwedo.html.

The Relationship between Existing Manuscripts and the Original Compositions

The documents we know as Matthew, Mark, Luke, and John were written sometime in the second half of the first century A.D. (I'll say more about the dating of the Gospels in chapter 4.) They were written on scrolls of papyrus (a rough, paper-like substance). Papyrus was popular because it was readily available and relatively inexpensive. But, unfortunately, it wasn't especially durable. Thus it is highly unlikely that any of the original Gospel manuscripts, called by the technical term *autographs*, exist today. Probably, the biblical autographs were worn out through use, though they could also have been misplaced by absentminded church leaders, destroyed by persecutors of the early Christians, or even eaten by critters.[3]

Because ancient documents tended to have a relatively short shelf life, people who valued them had a way of preserving their contents: copying. Professional copyists, called scribes, would copy the words of one text into a fresh papyrus or parchment (a longer lasting material made from animal skins). Their training taught the scribes to minimize errors and maximize accuracy.

Yet copying manuscripts was not a slavish task, with scribal accuracy matching modern photocopy technology. At times scribes would make intentional changes as they copied. For example, they would correct what they believed to be a spelling error in their source text. And even the best of scribes also sometimes made unintended errors. Thus the best extant[4] manuscripts of the Gospels are likely to differ in some measure from the autographs.

3. A fine discussion of how books were written in the time of early Christianity can be found in Bruce M. Metzger and Bart D. Ehrman, *The Text of the New Testament: Its Transmission, Corruption, and Restoration*, 4th ed. (Oxford: Oxford University Press, 2005). See pages 3–51, "The Making of Ancient Books."

4. "Extant" means "in existence today" and is frequently used by scholars to describe manuscripts that have not been lost or destroyed.

Moreover, it is probable that many of the first copies of the Gospels were made, not by professional scribes, but by literate lay copyists. As the early church rapidly expanded throughout the Roman world in the first centuries A.D., there was a pressing need for multiple copies of authoritative Christian documents, including Matthew, Mark, Luke, and John. Nonprofessional copyists must have stepped in to meet this need.

The fact that the original Gospel manuscripts have not survived to this day, combined with the fact that for centuries the text was passed on through a careful but imperfect process of copying, makes us wonder whether we can trust that the Greek text we have today looks anything like what the authors originally wrote down. Can we know what the original Gospel manuscripts actually said?

Standards for Evaluating the Reliability of Gospel Manuscripts

Before we examine the data, let's think for a moment about what might allow us to put confidence in the manuscripts of the Gospels.

First, we would look for *antiquity*. We'd want the manuscripts in existence to be old, the closer to the autographs the better. Less time between the original and an existing copy decreases the possibility of changes being introduced through many acts of copying.

Second, we would prefer *multiplicity*. Clearly, it would be better to have many manuscripts at our disposal rather than just a few. An abundance of manuscripts would put us in a much better position to determine the original wording.

Third, we would want *trustworthy scholarly methodology*. If the academics who study the biblical manuscripts, known as textual critics, utilize reliable methods, ones that maximize objectivity, then we would have greater confidence in their conclusions.

Fourth, we would look at the *quantity and quality of textually ambiguous passages* (made up of differences, called *variants,* among the manuscripts). If the existing copies of the Gospels contain a high proportion of textual variants, then we would question our ability to know what was originally written. If, on the contrary, the differences among extant manuscripts are relatively insignificant, then we would rightly place confidence in the critical Greek texts[5] upon which our translations are based.

So how does reality measure up to these standards?

The Antiquity of the Gospel Manuscripts

The oldest manuscript of the Gospels is a papyrus fragment of the Gospel of John. It is called P[52], text-critical shorthand for "Papyrus 52." This fragment, which contains part of Jesus' conversation with Pilate prior to the crucifixion (John 18:31–33, 37–38), has been dated to around A.D. 125. This means the copy of John of which P[52] is a tiny part was made within a couple of generations of the original writing of John's Gospel.[6] The next oldest manuscripts of the Gospels come from the latter part of the second century and the early part of the third century. P[4], P[45], P[64], P[66], P[67], and P[75] include significant portions of all four Gospels.

As we move further into the third century and beyond, we find many more extant manuscripts, including one of the most important parchment copies of the entire Bible, known as Codex Sinaiticus. This book was found in the mid-nineteenth century in a monastery near Mt. Sinai, from which it derives

---

5. "Critical Greek texts" are texts produced by teams of scholars working from the extant manuscripts of the New Testament. These scholars are called "text critics," and their discipline is called "text criticism." Critical Greek texts try to represent the original writing as closely as possible. Critical editions of the Greek New Testament also contain extensive footnotes to help scholars weigh differences among the various manuscripts.

6. For more detail about P[52] and the rest of the papyri, see Metzger and Ehrman, *Text of the New Testament,* 53–61.

its name. It has been dated to the fourth century A.D., and it contains the whole New Testament along with major sections of the Old Testament in Greek.[7]

How should we evaluate the antiquity of the Gospel manuscripts? The smallest time gap, the one between P[52] and the autograph of John's Gospel, is two generations. The more complete manuscripts are about a century later than the original writings, with extant copies of the whole New Testament more than two centuries later than the time of composition. From our point of view, the period between the extant manuscripts of the Gospels and the autographs may seem awfully long, and may raise doubts about the reliability of the Gospel manuscripts.

But if we compare the antiquity of the Gospel manuscripts with similar ancient writings, the case for trusting the Gospels gains considerable strength. Consider, for example, the writings of three historians more or less contemporaneous with the evangelists: the Jewish historian Josephus and the Roman historians Tacitus and Suetonius. The oldest extant manuscripts of Tacitus and Suetonius come from the ninth century.[8] Those of Josephus date back only to the eleventh century.[9] We're talking about a time gap of 800 to 1,000 years between the autographs and the extant manuscripts, yet historians accept the manuscripts as basically reliable representations of what was originally written. Lest it seem that I've chosen examples that are unusual, the oldest manuscripts of the classical historians Herodotus and Thucydides are separated from their autographs by about 500 years.[10]

If someone were to claim that we can't have confidence in the original content of the Gospels because the existing manuscripts

7. For the fascinating story of the discovery of Codex Sinaiticus, see ibid., 62–67.

8. J. Ed Komoszewski, M. James Sawyer, and Daniel B. Wallace, *Reinventing Jesus: What the Da Vinci Code and Other Novel Speculations Don't Tell You* (Grand Rapids, Mich.: Kregel, 2006), 71.

9. "Josephus," in *The Anchor Bible Dictionary*, David Noel Freedman, ed. (New York: Doubleday, 1992).

10. Komoszewski, Sawyer, and Wallace, *Reinventing Jesus*, 71.

are too far removed from the autographs, then that person would also have to cast doubt upon our knowledge of almost all ancient history and literature. Such skepticism, which is not found among classical scholars and historians, would be extreme and unwarranted.

Therefore, on the antiquity scale, the New Testament Gospels receive a top score.

The Multiplicity of the Gospel Manuscripts

Currently, scholars are aware of more than 5,700 manuscripts that contain some portion of the New Testament, and the total is growing slowly as additional manuscripts are discovered. Among these manuscripts, a couple thousand contain all or portions of the biblical Gospels.

Once again we should evaluate this total in light of comparable writings from the same period. What do we find if we look again at Tacitus, Suetonius, and Josephus? The histories of Tacitus exist today in three manuscripts, none of which contain all of his writings.[11] We're better off in the case of Suetonius, whose writings are found in more than 200 extant manuscripts. For Josephus we have 133 manuscripts.[12] Once again, if it seems like I'm stacking the deck in my own favor, there are 75 manuscripts of Herodotus, and only 20 of Thucydides.

The number of Gospel manuscripts in existence is about 20 times larger than the average number of extant manuscripts of comparable writings. I have not even considered the tens of thousands of manuscripts of Gospel translations into languages such as Latin and Syriac, many of which were made in the earliest centuries A.D. I have also not taken into account the hundreds of thousands of quotations of the Gospels found in the writings of early church leaders. Here's what Bruce Metzger and Bart Ehrman have to say about these citations:

11. Metzger and Ehrman, *Text of the New Testament*, 50–51.
12. Komoszewski, Sawyer, and Wallace, *Reinventing Jesus*, 71.

Besides textual evidence derived from the New Testament Greek manuscripts and from early versions, the textual critic has available the numerous scriptural quotations included in the commentaries, sermons, and other treatises written by early Church fathers. Indeed, so extensive are these citations that if all other sources for our knowledge of the text of the New Testament were destroyed, they would be sufficient alone for the reconstruction of practically the entire New Testament.[13]

After comparing the manuscripts of the New Testament with those for other ancient literature, Metzger and Ehrman conclude that "the textual critic of the New Testament is embarrassed by the wealth of material."[14]

The Reliability of Text-Critical Methodology

Yet this "wealth of material" also complicates the work of textual criticism. What methods do text critics use to determine the earliest form of the Gospel text?

First, they collect all of the known manuscripts, including ancient translations and writings of the early church fathers. The individual text critic doesn't actually do this alone, of course, but relies on the work of hundreds of other scholars, both present and past.

Second, text critics evaluate the manuscripts, looking for variants and seeking to determine which readings are the most likely to be original. They examine what is called *external evidence* and *internal evidence*. External evidence has to do with the number, antiquity, and relationships among the manuscripts. For example, if a variant is found in many, old manuscripts, then it is more reliable than one found in few, later manuscripts. Internal evidence concerns the actual content of the writing.

Though there is certainly a measure of subjectivity in text criticism, it is by far the most objective discipline in New Tes-

13. Metzger and Ehrman, *Text of the New Testament*, 126.
14. Ibid., 51.

tament studies. If you were to take two different teams of text critics and ask them to work independently on a critical edition of the Greek New Testament, they would agree more than 99 percent of the time. In fact, for the vast majority of words in the Gospels, text critics have come to an extremely high level of confidence concerning what was written in the autographs.

The Quantity and Quality of Textual Variants

Skeptics who try to cast doubt upon the reliability of the New Testament manuscripts point to the apparently large number of variants they contain. Bart Ehrman, for example, in *Misquoting Jesus*, suggests that there are 200,000 to 400,000 variants among the New Testament manuscripts. He adds, dramatically, "There are more variations among our manuscripts than there are words in the New Testament."[15] That sounds ominous, doesn't it? But, in fact, the data give us no reason to doubt the reliability of the manuscripts. Let me explain why.

We have such a large number of variants because there are so many extant manuscripts. Considering that the four Gospels contain a total of 64,000 words, and we have about 2,000 manuscripts of the Gospels, that's a lot of potential variants. But as I've already shown, having many manuscripts actually increases the likelihood of our getting back to the original text. It also adds to the number of variants, however, which can sound negative to one who isn't familiar with text-critical issues.

Let me suggest a more hypothetical example that might make clear what I'm saying. This book contains almost 50,000 words. Suppose I asked two people to make copies of this book by hand. Suppose, further, that they made one mistake every 1,000 words (99.9 percent accuracy). When they finished, each of their manuscripts would have 50 mistakes, for a total of 100. This doesn't sound too bad, does it? But suppose I asked

---

15. Bart D. Ehrman, *Misquoting Jesus: The Story behind Who Changed the Bible and Why* (New York: HarperSanFrancisco, 2005), 90.

2,000 people to make copies of my book. And suppose they also made a mistake every 1,000 words. When they finished, the total of mistakes in their manuscripts would be 100,000. This sounds like a lot of variants—more variants than words in my book, Bart Ehrman would say. But in fact the large number of variants is a simple product of the large number of manuscripts. Moreover, if text critics, lacking access to the original version (the autograph) of my book, were going to try and determine what my original version said, they'd be in a much stronger position if they had 2,000 copies to work from, even though they would be dealing with 100,000 variants. With 2,000 manuscripts, the text critics would be able to evaluate the variants more astutely and come up with something very close to what I originally wrote. If they had only two manuscripts, however, even though these included only 100 variants, they would find it harder to determine what the original manuscript said.

So, the fact "there are more variations among our manuscripts than there are words in the New Testament" isn't surprising. Nor is it bad news. It is a reflection of the wealth of the manuscript evidence available to us. The *actual number of variants* represents a tiny percentage of the variants that *could have occurred* among the manuscripts.

Moreover, the vast majority of variants in the New Testament manuscripts are insignificant, either because they appear so rarely that they are obviously not original, or because they don't appear in the older manuscripts, or because they don't impact the meaning of the text. In fact, the majority of variants that show up in enough older manuscripts to impact our reading of the text are spelling variations or errors.[16] Text critic Daniel Wallace concludes that "only about 1% of the textual variants" make any substantive difference.[17] And few, if any, of these have any bearing on theologically important matters. If you actually took out of the Gospels every word that was

16. Komoszewski, Sawyer, and Wallace, *Reinventing Jesus*, 56.
17. http://www.bible.org/page.asp?page_id=4000#P174_80529.

text-critically uncertain, the impact on your understanding of Jesus would be negligible.

Consider, for example, the two most obvious and significant textual variants in the Gospels. One of these appears in John 7:53–8:11, the story of the woman caught in adultery. Virtually all modern translations put this story in brackets, adding a note that says something like, "The earliest manuscripts do not include this passage." It's likely that this story is true, but that it was added to John well after the evangelist finished his task. Similarly, the ending of Mark includes a bracketed passage because the old manuscripts do not include anything after Mark 16:8. These two disputed passages, though significant in some ways, do not substantially alter our understanding of Jesus.

Do the Gospel Manuscripts Misquote Jesus?

At this point I should say a few words about Bart Ehrman's currently popular book *Misquoting Jesus*. Even when this book has fallen from the best-seller lists, its ideas will still be floating around in the cultural stream like bits of post-hurricane flotsam in the sea. (If you're looking for a more extensive critique of *Misquoting Jesus*, check what I've written on my web site,[18] as well as several excellent scholarly reviews.[19])

Ehrman's book is a popular introduction to textual criticism. When he sticks to objective descriptions, Ehrman's insights are both helpful and readable. For a scholar, he's an unusually effective popular communicator. Unfortunately, however, this book was not written merely to introduce people to textual criticism but also to undermine their confidence in the New Testament itself. I'm not reading between the

18. http://www.markdroberts.com/htmfiles/resources/biblequran.htm.
19. Daniel Wallace, "The Gospel according to Bart," http://www.bible.org/page.asp?page_id=4000#P174_80529; P. J. Williams, "Review of Misquoting Jesus," http://evangelicaltextualcriticism.blogspot.com/2005/12/review-of-bart-ehrman-misquoting-jesus_31.html; Craig L. Blomberg, "Review of *Misquoting Jesus*," http://www.denverseminary.edu/dj/articles2006/0200/0206.php.

lines here. Ehrman is very clear about his intentions from the beginning.[20]

One of the ironies of Ehrman's book is the title, *Misquoting Jesus*. You would expect to find a book full of instances in which the sayings of Jesus found in the Gospels were corrupted by the scribes. In fact, however, very little of the book is actually about misquoting Jesus. As Craig L. Blomberg says in his trenchant review, "the title appears designed to attract attention and sell copies of the book rather than to represent its contents accurately."[21]

Another irony comes when Ehrman talks about the number of variants among the New Testament manuscripts. As just noted, he says, "there are more variations among our manuscripts than there are words in the New Testament."[22] This startling sound bite appears to undermine the reliability of the manuscripts. But Ehrman also qualifies this observation. He writes:

> To be sure, of all the hundreds of thousands of textual changes found among our manuscripts, most of them are completely insignificant, immaterial, and of no real importance for anything other than showing that scribes could not spell or keep focused any better than the rest of us.[23]

> The changes [the scribes] made—at least the intentional ones—were no doubt seen as improvements of the text, possibly made because the scribes were convinced that the copyists before them had themselves mistakenly altered the words of the text. For the most part, their intention was to conserve the tradition, not to change it.[24]

One would expect to find these claims in a book touting the reliability of the New Testament manuscripts. Ehrman, in spite of his bias, is too good a scholar not to tell the truth here.

20. Ehrman, *Misquoting Jesus*, 10–15.
21. Blomberg, "Review of *Misquoting Jesus*."
22. Ehrman, *Misquoting Jesus*, 90, see also 11.
23. Ibid., 207.
24. Ibid., 215.

The greatest irony in *Misquoting Jesus* lies at the heart of Ehrman's argument against the trustworthiness of the manuscripts. The main point of his book is to undermine confidence in the New Testament on the ground that copyists changed the manuscripts, both intentionally and accidentally. One would expect Ehrman to put forth dozens of examples where we simply don't have any idea what the autographs actually said. Such repeated uncertainty would lead to the conclusion that we can't know with assurance what the New Testament writers, including the Gospel authors, actually wrote.

But, in fact, Ehrman's book is filled with examples that prove the opposite point. He does indeed offer many cases of textual variants. In virtually every case, Ehrman confidently explains what the change was, what the earlier manuscript actually said, and what motivated the copyist. In other words, Ehrman's book, though intending to weaken our certainty about the New Testament text, actually demonstrates how the abundance of manuscripts and the antiquity of manuscripts, when run through the mill of text-critical methodology, allow us to know with a very high level of probability what the evangelists and other New Testament authors wrote. This might explain why there are many textual critics who are committed Christians with an evangelical view of Scripture.[25]

Conclusion

Can we know what the original Gospel manuscripts really said? Yes, we can. We can have confidence that the critical Greek texts of Matthew, Mark, Luke, and John represent, with a very high degree of probability, what the autographs of the Gospels actually contained.

---

25. See, for example, the text critics associated with the Evangelical Textual Criticism web site: http://evangelicaltextualcriticism.blogspot.com/.

Chapter 3

Did the Evangelists Know Jesus Personally?

Most Christians believe that two of the Gospels were written by people who knew Jesus personally: the first Gospel, by Matthew; and the fourth Gospel, by John. The titles of these Gospels appear to reveal their authorship: "The Gospel According to *Matthew*" and "The Gospel According to *John*." And Jesus is known to have had disciples named Matthew and John. So when scholars start wondering if Matthew and John really wrote these Gospels, people get bugged. Why can't scholars leave well enough alone?

Moreover, there's something appealing about the idea that the first Gospel reflects Matthew's immediate experience of Jesus and the fourth Gospel John's intimate knowledge of the Lord. This relational dynamic makes the Gospels seem more personal and less didactic. Furthermore, authorship by Matthew and John seems to increase the likelihood of both Gospels being historically accurate. And, since they overlap considerably with the other two Gospels, the historicity of the second and third Gospels gets a boost from the witness of Matthew and John. Authorship of the Gospels by eyewitnesses of Jesus doesn't guarantee historical accuracy, of course, because people can misrepresent what they know, or they can forget, or remember imprecisely. But it certainly feels better to know that Matthew and John really knew Jesus, even if Mark and Luke did not.

You won't be surprised to learn that many scholars doubt these traditional views of Gospel authorship. They don't believe any of the Gospels were written by one of "the Twelve." Yet, given the tendency of much modern scholarship to be overly skeptical, you may be pleasantly surprised to learn that quite a few scholars believe that the Gospels, if not actually written by one of Jesus' disciples, nevertheless reflect genuine reminiscences by these disciples.

Evidence for Gospel Authorship

The basic problem we face when it comes to the authorship of the Gospels is that they are anonymous, or at least they were at first. There's no evidence to suggest that whoever wrote Matthew entitled his narrative about Jesus: "The Gospel According to Matthew." Ditto with the other biblical Gospels. It wasn't until sometime in the second century that scribes began to put the names "Matthew," "Mark," "Luke," and "John" alongside the Gospels supposedly written by them.

Ironically, the Gospels that do often include a named author are the noncanonical varieties. *The Gospel of Thomas*, for example, begins: "These are the secret sayings which the living Jesus spoke and which Didymos Judas Thomas wrote down." Almost no scholar believes that the extrabiblical Gospels were actually written by their purported authors. They are pseudonymous (falsely named) rather than anonymous. I'll have more to say about the significance of this distinction later in the chapter.

40

Similar to what we saw in the case of textual criticism, the evidence for Gospel authorship falls into two categories: external evidence and internal evidence. External evidence is testimony from the early church about who wrote the Gospels. Internal evidence is that which can be gleaned from the texts of the Gospels themselves (or, in the case of Luke, from Acts as well, since the same author wrote both Luke and Acts).

External Evidence for Gospel Authorship

In the second century A.D. it became common to identify the authors of the New Testament Gospels as Matthew, Mark, Luke, and John. By early in the third century these identifications were solidly entrenched. We can't be sure exactly how the tradition developed in the second century, but we can note a few significant signposts along the way.

Around A.D. 180, Irenaeus, the bishop of Lugundum in Roman Gaul (now Lyons, France), wrote a treatise defending orthodox Christianity against a wide spectrum of supposedly Christian but, in Irenaeus's perspective, unacceptable theologies. In *Against Heresies*, Irenaeus specifically mentioned Matthew, Mark, Luke, and John as the authors of the Gospels. For example, in one section of his work Irenaeus wrote:

> Matthew also issued a written Gospel among the Hebrews in their own dialect, while Peter and Paul were preaching at Rome, and laying the foundations of the Church. After their departure, Mark, the disciple and interpreter of Peter, did also hand down to us in writing what had been preached by Peter. Luke also, the companion of Paul, recorded in a book the Gospel preached by him. Afterwards, John, the disciple of the Lord, who also had leaned upon His breast, did himself publish a Gospel during his residence at Ephesus in Asia.[1]

1. Irenaeus, *Against Heresies* 3.1.1; see also 3.11.8–9. The translation is from Alexander Roberts and James Donaldson, eds., *The Ante-Nicene Fathers*, reprint ed. (Grand Rapids, Mich.: Eerdmans, 1978–1980).

Given the brevity of this paragraph and the lack of explanation, it seems that these traditions had already been well established in the church circles in which Irenaeus was a leader.

About a decade before Irenaeus wrote *Against Heresies* some anonymous early Christian compiled a list of authoritative writings. The Muratorian Canon, named after the person who published it in 1740, refers to four Gospels, though the manuscript no longer contains the specifics concerning the first two. It does mention Luke and John by name:

> . . . at which nevertheless he was present, and so he placed [them in his narrative]. The third book of the Gospel is that according to Luke. Luke, the well-known physician, after the ascension of Christ, when Paul had taken with him as one zealous for the law, composed it in his own name, according to [the general] belief. Yet he himself had not seen the Lord in the flesh; and therefore, as he was able to ascertain events, so indeed he begins to tell the story from the birth of John. The fourth of the Gospels is that of John, [one] of the disciples. . . .[2]

It's interesting to note that Luke is identified explicitly as one who was not an eyewitness to Jesus.

The earliest bit of external evidence for Gospel authorship comes from a church leader who served during the first half of the second century. About fifty years before Irenaeus, a bishop named Papias, who lived in Hierapolis (now in western Turkey), wrote a document called *Expositions of the Oracles of the Lord*. This document doesn't exist anymore, but it is quoted in other early Christian writings that we do have today. One of these quotations appears in the writings of the church historian Eusebius:

> Mark having become the interpreter of Peter, wrote down accurately, though not in order, whatsoever he remembered of the things said or done by Christ. For he neither heard the Lord

---

2. Quoted in Lee M. McDonald, *The Formation of the Christian Biblical Canon: Revised and Expanded Edition* (Peabody, Mass.: Hendrickson, 1995), 209–210.

nor followed him, but afterward, as I said, he followed Peter, who adapted his teaching to the needs of his hearers, but with no intention of giving a connected account of the Lord's discourses, so that Mark committed no error while he thus wrote some things as he remembered them. For he was careful of one thing, not to omit any of the things which he had heard, and not to state any of them falsely. . . . So then Matthew wrote the oracles in the Hebrew language, and every one interpreted them as he was able.[3]

I'll have more to say about this statement later. For now I simply want to note that by about A.D. 130 the tradition of Matthew's and Mark's authorship was being passed down authoritatively, since Papias claims to have received this information from an unidentified "elder."

For various reasons, however, many scholars doubt the accuracy of the second-century traditions about Gospel authorship. This is true even though the ancient tradition is almost unanimous in attributing the Gospels to Matthew, Mark, Luke, and John. Scholarly doubts about Gospel authorship usually have to do with internal evidence, what the Gospels themselves reveal about who wrote them (or not).

Internal Evidence for Gospel Authorship

Most of the internal evidence for Gospel authorship is fairly speculative. It involves such questions as:

Does the apparent reliance of the first Gospel on the second Gospel count against the theory that Matthew, a disciple of Jesus, wrote the first Gospel? Would he have based his work on the writing of somebody who didn't even know Jesus personally?

---

3. Quoted in Eusebius, *Church History* 3.39.15–16. The translation is from Philip Schaff and Henry Wace, eds., *A Select Library of Nicene and Post-Nicene Fathers*, 2nd series (Grand Rapids, Mich.: Eerdmans, 1952–1957).

Since the vocabulary of the second Gospel includes Latinisms (Latin terms in a Greek text—for example: *legion* in 5:9; *denarius* in 6:37; *centurion* in 15:39), does this support the notion that the author was writing in a location where Latin was the primary language, such as Rome, and thus that he might have been Mark, Peter's companion in Rome?

Since the theology of the third Gospel (plus Acts) seems to differ from that of Paul in some respects, is it sensible to believe that the author of these writings had been a close companion of Paul?

Does the presence of lots of authentic local color in the fourth Gospel support authorship by John?

As you can see, there's a lot of wiggle room in questions like these. The same is true for most of the internal evidence for the identity of the evangelists.

There are two pieces of internal evidence which, it seems to me, deserve serious consideration. One has to do with the authorship of the third Gospel, the other with the authorship of the fourth Gospel.

Was the Author of the Third Gospel a Companion of Paul?

Second-century Christian tradition ascribes the authorship of the third Gospel to Luke, a companion of Paul. Indeed, a person named Luke is mentioned in three of Paul's letters (Philem. 24; Col. 4:14; 2 Tim. 4:11). Colossians adds that Luke is the "beloved physician" (Col. 4:14).

Internal evidence for Luke's authorship of the third Gospel comes primarily from the Acts of the Apostles, which was written by the author of the third Gospel (compare Luke 1:1–4 and Acts 1:1–5). There are passages in Acts where the author speaks as if he were a companion of Paul during some of his journeys (for example, Acts 16:10–17). Piecing these clues and others together, commentators have for centuries concluded that Luke was this companion of Paul, and therefore was the author both of Acts and the third Gospel. Many scholars today believe this is a credible inference, while others deny it, largely on the basis of supposed differences between Luke's theology and Paul's theology, and because the "we" sections in Acts are seen as a literary device, not as evidence that the author of Acts was truly a companion of Paul.

If the connection between Luke and Paul can be made, this does increase the feeling of Luke's overall trustworthiness. His writings have an apostolic imprimatur, as it were. But, of course, the curious thing about this connection is that Paul never knew Jesus during his earthly life. So linking Luke with Paul, though it might increase Luke's general believability, doesn't provide evidence of how Luke knew the truth about Jesus.

Was the Author of the Fourth Gospel John, the Disciple of Jesus?

The most obvious, yet still tantalizingly cryptic, internal evidence for a writer of a New Testament Gospel comes in the fourth Gospel. This Gospel actually makes reference to its writer near the end of the book:

> Peter turned and saw the disciple whom Jesus loved following them; he was the one who had reclined next to Jesus at the supper and had said, "Lord, who is it that is going to betray you?" When Peter saw him, he said to Jesus, "Lord, what about him?" Jesus said to him, "If it is my will that he remain until I come, what is that to you? Follow me!" So the rumor spread in the community that this disciple would not die. Yet Jesus did not say to him that he would not die, but, "If it is my will that he remain until I come, what is that to you?" This is the disciple who is testifying to these things and has written them, and we know that his testimony is true (John 21:20–24).

45

This passage appears to identify the writer of the Gospel, though the Greek phrase behind "has written them" could mean "has caused them to be written," which would identify the disciple as the inspiration for the writing of the fourth Gospel but not necessarily its actual author. Moreover, the phrase "we know that his testimony is true" suggests that others were involved in the writing and/or editing of the fourth Gospel, at least to some extent.

The text of the fourth Gospel identifies the primary author of the book as "this . . . disciple," namely, "the disciple whom Jesus loved." This identification points to one of the great mysteries of biblical interpretation: Who is the Beloved Disciple?

Given Jesus' love for all of his disciples, the phrase "the disciple whom Jesus loved" seems peculiar. Nevertheless, it appears elsewhere in the fourth Gospel. The one known as the Beloved Disciple reclined with Jesus at the Last Supper (13:23), stayed with him as he was crucified (19:26), ran to the tomb on Easter morning (20:2), and joined the resurrected Jesus at the Sea of Galilee (21:7, 20). Traditionally, he has been seen as John, the son of Zebedee, though this identification is never made explicitly in the fourth Gospel itself. What is claimed, however, is that the one who wrote (or whose testimony stood behind) the fourth Gospel was a disciple of Jesus, one whom Jesus dearly loved. This could well have been John, though surely Jesus might have loved another disciple, someone whose name we don't know. For example, Ben Witherington III has presented intriguing arguments in favor of Lazarus as the Beloved Disciple.[4] This identification is supported by the fact that Lazarus is specifically and unusually described as one who was loved by Jesus (11:3, 5, 11, 36).

For our purposes, it doesn't really matter whether the Beloved Disciple was John, Lazarus, or some other disciple of Jesus. The important point is that the fourth Gospel claims to contain the writing of someone who was a close follower of

---

4. Ben Witherington III, *What Have They Done with Jesus? Beyond Strange Theories and Bad History* (New York: HarperSanFrancisco, 2006), 127–152.

Jesus. If this is true, then it surely increases the trustworthiness of the fourth Gospel.

Some scholars have doubted this conclusion because the content of Jesus' teaching in the fourth Gospel is so different from what we find in the Synoptic Gospels. When it comes to the basic forms of discourse, this is surely true. In the Synoptics Jesus usually utters short statements or parables. In the fourth Gospel, he speaks in long discourses. Moreover, the central point of Jesus' teaching in the Synoptic Gospels is the kingdom of God. In John, the kingdom is a minor theme. Jesus emphasizes far more his personal identity and the need to believe in him.

Nobody disputes the variations between the fourth Gospel and the Synoptic Gospels with respect to form and content. Yet there is a wide difference of opinion over the implications of this variance. Some scholars focus so much on the differences between the Synoptics and the fourth Gospel that they seem to overlook the extensive thematic similarities shared among them. Christians throughout the centuries have seen in the fourth Gospel a picture of Jesus complementary to the one found in the Synoptics.[5] I'll have more to say about the differences and similarities between the fourth Gospel and the Synoptics in chapter 8. For now, let me conclude simply by saying that I find no compelling reason to reject the idea that the fourth Gospel was written by someone who had been one of Jesus' closest disciples, and many reasons to accept this idea.

Summing Up the Question of Gospel Authorship

Most of the internal evidence for Gospel authorship, apart from the identification of the Beloved Disciple, is quite speculative. Even the identity of the Beloved Disciple cannot be known

---

5. For an in-depth analysis of the relationship between John and the Synoptics, in the context of a defense of the historicity of John, see Craig L. Blomberg, *The Historical Reliability of John's Gospel: Issues and Commentary* (Downers Grove, Ill.: InterVarsity Press, 2001).

with certainty. Scholarly opinion, therefore, rests largely on the weight given to the second-century traditions. Those who think that Irenaeus, Papias, and the rest knew and passed on the truth tend to affirm traditional views of Gospel authorship. Those who doubt these traditions argue for more anonymity.

Why, you might wonder, would a scholar in the twenty-first century doubt the traditions that go back into the second century? Doesn't it make sense to think that those early traditions were based on actual testimony? Wouldn't you suppose that those who passed along the Gospels also passed along information about who actually wrote them?

All of this seems quite reasonable, unless you approach the tradition with a hermeneutic of suspicion, in which the claims made by church leaders are presumed to be "guilty until proven innocent." Quite a few scholars have argued that the names of the Gospel writers were made up in order to gain authority for the writings. This is surely true when you consider the broader collection of Christian (or semi-Christian) Gospels. In the noncanonical writings you find such documents as the *Gospel of Thomas*, the *Gospel of Philip*, the *Gospel of Mary* (Magdalene), the *Gospel of Judas*, the *Gospel of Bartholomew*, the *Gospel of Peter*, as well as many others. It's clear to almost all observers that these books were not actually written by the supposed authors. The names were attached to give authority to the writings. So, some have concluded, the same is true of the New Testament Gospels.

This argument *could* explain the naming of Matthew and John, though I think it reflects unwarranted skepticism about early Christian tradition. But the main flaw in this argument is obvious: *Two of the biblical Gospels were named after relatively inconsequential characters who did not actually know Jesus in the flesh.* If you were some second-century Christian wanting to make up an author for a Gospel, you would never choose Mark, even if he was believed to have been a companion of Peter. And you would never choose Luke because he had no direct connection to Jesus at all, even though he played a bit part in the writings of Paul. If second-century Christians were fabricating traditional authorship for the canonical Gospels, surely they could have done a better job.

So, ironically, the tendency of the noncanonical Gospels to assign Gospel authorship to prominent disciples actually *increases* the likelihood that the traditions concerning New Testament Gospel authorship are true, at least with respect to Mark and Luke. And if the orthodox tradition can be seen as trustworthy in these cases, then the presumption of suspicion about the tradition must be wrongheaded. We should accept the ancient tradition unless we have good reason to do otherwise. Moreover, the *anonymity* of the biblical Gospels bears the stamp of truth whereas the *pseudonymity* of the noncanonical Gospels suggests their falsehood.

Did the Gospel writers know Jesus personally? With confidence, we can say "no" in the cases of the second and third Gospels. But these evangelists had access to reliable traditions about Jesus, as I'll explain later. Moreover, the fact that the second Gospel was so quickly accepted by the early church (including the other evangelists) lends credence to the notion that it was based on reliable source(s), like Peter, as Papias claimed.

In the case of the first and fourth Gospels, it is possible that the writers were eyewitnesses of Jesus himself. There was a time when critical scholars seemed to discard this possibility energetically, almost glibly. But in recent years many have come to believe that the first and fourth Gospels reflect the memory and the perspective of Jesus' own disciples, both Matthew and John (or another Beloved Disciple, at any rate). Matthew and John may not have been the ones who finally put pen to papyrus, but they, their memory, and their authority stand behind the Gospels that bear their names.

So, did the Gospel writers know Jesus personally? Mark and Luke did not. Matthew and John might have, but we can't be positive. *Yet the reliability of the New Testament Gospels does not depend on who wrote them so much as on the nature and purpose of the writings themselves.* These matters fill out the rest of this book, in which I will use the traditional names to identify the Gospels and their writers.

Mark, Luke, and the Early Christian Commitment to Truth

I want to conclude this chapter by reflecting a bit further on the traditional assignment of the second and third Gospels to Mark and Luke. Early Christian tradition is unified in the identification of Mark and Luke as Gospel writers. It also contains specific notice that these two evangelists did not know Jesus personally.

I already mentioned how striking it is that the orthodox church "settled" for such unspectacular writers. After all, their theological opponents, the Gnostics, were making all sorts of claims that *their* Gospels and other revelations came from the original disciples of Jesus. It must have been tempting for the orthodox believers to counter these claims by connecting their Gospels with more authoritative writers who had actually been with Jesus. Why not exaggerate just a bit and call the second Gospel the Gospel of Peter, even though it was written by his associate and not by Peter himself? Yet Papias, Irenaeus, and the like resolutely refused to do this sort of thing. In fact, they openly acknowledged that two of their Gospels were not written by eyewitnesses.

I've suggested that this strongly supports the theory that Mark and Luke were the writers of the second and third Gospels. But, in a broader perspective, the refusal of early orthodox Christians to fudge on the question of Gospel authorship reveals their commitment to truth. They steadfastly affirmed what they believed to be true, even when their opponents appeared to trump Mark and Luke with Gospels by Thomas, Philip, and the like. The orthodox dedication to truth won out over any supposed orthodox agenda to uphold the true faith versus Gnosticism.

I am belaboring this point because among many scholars who discount the historical reliability of the Gospels you'll find an assumption that the early Christians made up all sorts of things when it supported their evangelistic or apologetic agendas. Need a miracle story to compete with pagan gods? Make it up! Need a saying of Jesus to advance your cause? Go ahead and create one! In many scholarly quarters the creativity of the early Christian movement with respect to Jesus is assumed without argument.

I am not claiming that second-century attribution of Gospels to Mark and Luke proves that Christians never made anything up. This would be to claim more than the evidence supports at this point. But I do think the consistent testimony of authorship by Mark and Luke offers a clear instance in which orthodox Christians might have been tempted to bend the truth to fit their agenda yet in which they resolutely hung on to the truth. This would suggest that scholars who neglect the early Christian commitment to truth have missed the truth themselves.

Chapter 4

When Were the Gospels Written?

Everybody seems to be talking about the Gospels these days, and not just the biblical Gospels but especially the noncanonical ones. The shelves of secular bookstores feature books promising to reveal the secrets of the hidden Gospels. For the first time in history, the Gnostic Gospels named after Mary and Philip have emerged from hiding in musty academic libraries, owing to their cameo appearance in *The Da Vinci Code*. Then there was the publication of the *Gospel of Judas*, accompanied with blaring media fanfare and insinuations by scholars that we might finally have access to the truth about the relationship between Judas and Jesus. No doubt there will be more of the same in the years to come.

Much of today's babble about the Gospels seems to assume that they are all more or less of equal historical value. If something's called a Gospel, people figure, it must give us authentic information about Jesus, no matter where it came from or when it was written. Some folks have even argued that the extrabiblical Gospels are better historical sources than Matthew, Mark, Luke, and John. *The Da Vinci Code*'s fictitious Sir Leigh Teabing is the most popular proponent of this view, but he's not alone.[1]

Although parts of this discussion have been academically responsible, it reminds me of a story I heard from one of my college philosophy professors. I had asked Hillary Putnam, "What is the strangest paper you've ever received in one of your courses?"

Without hesitation he answered, "It was in a modern philosophy class I taught several years ago. A student submitted a term paper comparing the philosophies of John Locke [a seventeenth-century English philosopher] and Jean-Paul Sartre [a twentieth-century French philosopher]. He found some notable parallels between Locke and Sartre. Unfortunately, however, his main thesis was that Locke had borrowed many of his key ideas from Sartre. This student had never bothered to find out that Sartre came along *almost three centuries after Locke*."

So it is with much of the popular conversation about the Gospels. People are making claims that are almost laughable, except for the fact that they seem to believe them, as do others who are unaware of when the Gospels were written.

In this chapter I plan to answer two main questions:

1. When were the biblical Gospels written?
2. What do the dates of composition for the Gospels—both biblical and noncanonical—tell us about their trustworthiness as historical sources?

---

1. The Jesus Seminar is well known for its preference for the *Gospel of Thomas* as a historical source for Jesus. My dissertation advisor, Helmut Koester, is the most prolific serious scholar to defend the historical value of the noncanonical Gospels. See, for example, Helmut Koester, *Ancient Christian Gospels: Their History and Development* (Philadelphia: Trinity Press International, 1990).

When Were the Biblical Gospels Written?

The dating of the Gospels involves a generous helping of subjectivity and therefore leads to considerable disagreement among scholars. The main problem is a lack of evidence. The evangelists didn't identify when they were writing, adding a preface that might read something like, "In the twelfth year of the reign of the Emperor Nero . . ." So, the dating of the New Testament Gospels is rather like a treasure hunt, with scholars searching high and low for relevant clues.

These clues fall into two categories that will, by now, sound familiar. First, there is *external evidence*. This includes the early manuscripts of the Gospels as well as references to them or citations from them in other works of ancient literature. Second, there is *internal evidence*. This has to do with what can be discovered about the time of writing from the content of each Gospel. Consider this obvious example. All of the Gospels identify Pontius Pilate as the Roman governor of Judea during the time of Jesus. Since we know that Pilate governed from about 26 to 37 A.D., the Gospels couldn't have been written before this time.

External Evidence for the Dating of the Gospels

As I explained in chapter 2, there are papyrus manuscripts of the biblical Gospels that can be dated to the last part of the second century A.D. Therefore the originals must have been written earlier. For John we have P^{52}, which has been dated to around A.D. 125, thus ensuring that this Gospel was written no later than the first part of the second century.[2]

---

2. Some scholars have suggested that fragments of Mark's Gospel were found in the Judean caves that once hid the Dead Sea Scrolls. These fragments, dated to around A.D. 50, would support an early date for the writing of Mark. But most experts have not endorsed this theory, partly because the fragments are too small for definitive conclusions. See the discussion by William L. Lane in *The Gospel of Mark* (Grand Rapids, Mich.: Eerdmans, 1974), 18–21.

Besides the extant manuscripts, we find references to the Gospels in writings by second-century church leaders. Irenaeus, who wrote his treatise *Against Heresies* around A.D. 180, specifically mentioned Matthew, Mark, Luke, and John as being the only authoritative Gospels.[3] His description of the evangelists puts their writing in the latter half of the first century A.D. *Against Heresies* establishes a latest possible date for the composition of the Gospels and suggests that they were in fact written quite a bit earlier. The Muratorian Canon, written perhaps ten years before Irenaeus, mentions Luke and John by name, and probably included Matthew and Mark as well.

A half-century before Irenaeus, Papias said that Mark wrote down things that Peter taught about Jesus, and that Matthew compiled reports about Jesus "in the Hebrew language."[4] It seems likely that Papias is referring to what we know as the Gospel of Mark, and perhaps to the Gospel of Matthew. If so, then we have a reliable latest possible date for the writing of Mark and maybe Matthew: prior to A.D. 130 or so, when Papias wrote. Moreover, what Papias said about these Gospels dates their authorship to the first century.

There are no earlier references to the biblical Gospels, but there are possible quotations of the Gospels in Christian writings from the first decade of the second century. Ignatius, Bishop of Antioch, while on his way to Rome to be martyred, wrote several letters in which he seems to have quoted from Matthew.[5] The so-called *Didache* ("teaching" in Greek), written around the same time, also shows what might be knowledge of Matthew.[6] If the passages in Ignatius and the Didache are indeed quotations from Matthew, and not simply reflections of oral tradition, then we have external evidence for Matthew's having been written by the end of the first century A.D.

3. Irenaeus, *Against Heresies* 3.1.1; 3.11.8–9.
4. Quoted in Eusebius, *Church History* 3.39.15–16.
5. For details, see D. A. Carson and Douglas J. Moo, *An Introduction to the New Testament*, 2nd ed. (Grand Rapids, Mich.: Zondervan, 2005), 152.
6. Raymond E. Brown, *An Introduction to the New Testament* (New York: Doubleday, 1997), 216.

The most extensive quotation of the Gospels comes from the Gospels themselves. As I'll explain in the next chapter, most scholars believe that Matthew and Luke used Mark as a source for their writing. If this is true, then Mark must have been written before either of these Gospels, and early enough to have been known by both writers. This pushes the writing of Mark near the middle of the first century A.D.

Internal Evidence for the Dating of the Gospels

Scholarly arguments from internal evidence abound. If you're interested in the details, check out any commentary on the Gospels or a standard New Testament introduction.[7] Most of these arguments try to squeeze chronological water from very dry stones, however. The best analyses try to "fit" the Gospels into what is known about early Christian history. For example, the Gospel of John seems to reflect a time when Christians and Jews were experiencing considerable conflict. This suggests a date in the last two decades of the first century A.D. But, of course, the fourth Gospel may have been written earlier in a community where conflict with Jews happened locally before it became a widespread phenomenon. "Good fit" arguments depend on lots of historical reconstruction that is probable at best.[8]

The most common arguments for dating the Gospels based on internal evidence refer to the fall of Jerusalem and the destruction of the temple in A.D. 70. This was, no doubt, a cataclysmic event for many early Christians, especially those who continued to think of themselves as Jews. Scholars examine the Gospels for evidence of knowledge—or lack of knowledge—of

7. I would recommend two New Testament introductions. For a more conservative approach, see Carson and Moo, *Introduction to the New Testament*. For a responsible survey of scholarship from a non-evangelical point of view, see Brown, *Introduction to the New Testament*.

8. The best recent overview of first-century Christian history is found in Ben Witherington III, *New Testament History: A Narrative Account* (Grand Rapids, Mich.: Baker, 2001).

the events of A.D. 70. You can find some commentators who argue that the Gospels reflect no specific knowledge of these events, and therefore must be dated prior to 70. Yet you'll find others who see between the lines of the Gospels ample references to the fall of Jerusalem, and therefore date all of the Gospels after 70. For my own part, I find some of the arguments for earlier dating enticing, but not so compelling as to convince me that they are correct. All of these kinds of positions are filled with conjecture about what an evangelist "surely would have said" or "might have meant." These arguments offer packed sand upon which to date the Gospels, but hardly a rock-solid foundation.[9]

Accepted Dates of Composition

If you were to do a survey of New Testament scholarship today, you would find the majority of scholars falling somewhere within the following ranges for the dating of the Gospels:

Matthew: 65–85 A.D.
Mark: 60–75 A.D.
Luke: 65–95 A.D.
John: 75–100 A.D.

If these accepted ranges are accurate, then the biblical Gospels were written around 30–70 years after the death of Jesus.

Does this time lapse help us trust the Gospels? Before I answer this question, I need to address two other issues. First, I should comment on how the dating of the biblical Gospels compares with the dating of their extrabiblical cousins. I'll

9. For the dating of the Gospel of Luke, we have additional evidence because of its obvious connection with the Acts of the Apostles. The introductions to both books (Luke 1:1–4; Acts 1:1–5) and the common style of writing strongly suggest one writer for both volumes. Thus if one can date Acts on the basis of internal data, one gets a date for Luke for free, as it were. Unfortunately, proposals for the dating of Acts range widely, and do not offer compelling proof of the time when Luke was written.

address this in just a moment. Second, I need to explain in some detail how the evangelists got their information about Jesus. Did they depend upon their own memories? Did they make it up as they went along? Or did they use reliable sources? This discussion I'll save for the next two chapters.

When Were the Noncanonical Gospels Written?

The noncanonical Gospels are ancient writings in which Jesus (or an otherworldly Christ, at any rate) sometimes figures prominently. A few of the extrabiblical Gospels purport to describe events in the life of Jesus. An example would be the *Infancy Gospel of Thomas*, which supposedly chronicles miracles by the boy Jesus. Most of the noncanonical Gospels, especially those known as the Gnostic Gospels because of their theology, say almost nothing about the human Jesus. Instead, they contain what are portrayed as secret revelations from the divine Christ. *The Gospel of Thomas* exemplifies this type of writing. Other Gnostic Gospels, like the *Gospel of Truth*, are theological tractates that have little to do directly with Christ. Depending on what you count as a Gospel, there are two or three dozen noncanonical Gospels. For the most part, these can be found in what is called the New Testament Apocrypha[10] or the Nag Hammadi Library.[11] If we have little evidence for conclusive dating of the canonical Gospels, the situation with the noncanonicals is even less helpful. In some cases we have external evidence for dating. Irenaeus, for example, mentions a *Gospel of Truth* that may be the same as the one found in the Nag Hammadi Library.[12] He rejects its authority, of course. For the most part, however, external evidence for the noncanonical Gospels is minimal.

10. See Wilhelm Schneemelcher, ed., *New Testament Apocrypha*, trans. R. McL. Wilson (Louisville: Westminster/John Knox, 1991).

11. James M. Robinson, ed., *The Nag Hammadi Library in English* (New York: Harper & Row, 1977).

12. Irenaeus, *Against Heresies* 3.11.9.

Internal evidence often relates to the dependence of the noncanonical Gospels upon the biblical versions. Many of the extrabiblical Gospels quote from Matthew, Mark, Luke, and John, and often from other New Testament writings as well, such as the letters of Paul. Such quotations don't allow for a precise dating of the noncanonical documents, but they do indicate that they were written after the biblical books being quoted.

Most scholars put the composition of all the noncanonical Gospels in the second century A.D. or later, with one exception that I'll address in a moment. At the latter end of the scale you would find the *Gospel of Philip*, which was composed during the last part of the second century or the first part of the third century. Other texts, such as the *Gospel of Truth* and the *Gospel of Mary*, are believed to have been written earlier in the second century.

The one major exception to the "noncanonicals in the second century" rule is the *Gospel of Thomas*. Perhaps no Gospel has enjoyed a wider range of possible dates. Some scholars have tried to place the composition of *Thomas* to within twenty years of Jesus' ministry, while others argue that this Gospel was written well into the second century. Careful comparisons between *Thomas* and the biblical Gospels have made a strong case for the latter date, and I'm inclined to agree.[13] They show how *Thomas* is dependent upon a range of biblical writings, and thus must have been written well after those writings were composed.[14]

13. K. R. Snodgrass, "The Gospel of Thomas: A Secondary Gospel," *Second Century* 7 (1989–1990): 19–38; C. M. Tuckett, "Thomas and the Synoptics," *Novum Testamentum* 30 (1988): 132–157; C. A. Evans, "Thomas, Gospel of," in *Dictionary of the Later New Testament and Its Developments*, ed. Ralph P. Martin and P. H. Davids (Downers Grove, Ill.: InterVarsity Press, 1997), 1175–1177.

14. Ironically, however, an early date for *Thomas* would actually work in favor of the canonical Gospels, since the bulk of *Thomas* consists of sayings of Jesus that are found in the biblical Gospels. If *Thomas* were early, then it would provide independent attestation for the authenticity of much of what we find in the canonical Gospels. I once accepted an early date for *Thomas*, but the writers in the previous footnotes have caused me to question my earlier judgment. Thanks to Ben Witherington for pointing me to these writers.

What Do the Dates of Composition for the Gospels Tell Us about Their Trustworthiness?

Usually we would put more confidence in a historical description that was closer to an event than in a later testimony, especially when the later testimony was dependent on the earlier source. Therefore, we can conclude that the biblical Gospels are more trustworthy as historical sources for Jesus than the noncanonical Gospels, though these later Gospels might sometimes contain bits and pieces of authentic tradition that are not found in the Bible.

But as I noted earlier, the writing of the biblical Gospels happened two or three generations after Jesus' ministry. This time gap makes us wonder what the evangelists depended on when they wrote. Were they relying on memory? On written descriptions? On hearsay? What happened with stories about Jesus during the years after his ministry and before the writing of the Gospels? To these questions we'll turn in the next chapter.

Chapter 5

What Sources Did
the Gospel Writers Use?

Good sources are treasure for historians. Even when writing about an event they experienced personally, careful historians will consult sources beyond their personal knowledge. They'll interview other witnesses. They'll comb through published accounts. This is what responsible historiography always entails.

As I explained in chapter 3, at least two of the Gospel writers were not eyewitnesses of Jesus. The other two, Matthew and John, may well have been among Jesus' inner circle, but we can't be positive about this. What we do know for sure is that at least one of the evangelists made up for his lack of direct knowledge of Jesus by carefully collecting and utilizing historical sources. We know this because Luke tells us right up front.

Luke and His Sources

The Gospel of Luke begins with a prologue similar to something an ancient historian would have written:

> Since many have undertaken to set down an orderly account of the events that have been fulfilled among us, just as they were handed on to us by those who from the beginning were eyewitnesses and servants of the word, I too decided, after investigating everything carefully from the very first, to write an orderly account for you, most excellent Theophilus, so that you may know the truth concerning the things about which you have been instructed (Luke 1:1–4).

We don't know who Theophilus was, though apparently he knew Luke and was willing to receive instruction from him. Theophilus may have been Luke's patron (financial supporter), perhaps a newer Christian who looked up to Luke.

Our interest lies chiefly in the sources Luke identifies. Notice carefully what he claims:

1. "Many" have already "set down an orderly account" of the events concerning Jesus. The phrase "set down an orderly account" refers to writing a narrative. Luke consciously drew upon more than one or two written sources.

2. The events concerning Jesus "were handed on to us by those who from the beginning were eyewitnesses and servants of the word." "Handed on" is the language of oral tradition. It conveys the intentional passing on of stories and sayings. "Eyewitnesses" are those who actually saw and heard Jesus in the flesh. "Servants of the word" are those who preached and taught. So Luke attests to a thriving oral tradition about Jesus which was passed on by preachers and teachers. Yet these were not just any old servants of the word. Luke paid particular attention to those who based their preaching and teaching on their own eyewitness experience of Jesus.

3. Luke decided to write his Gospel "after investigating everything carefully." In other words, he read the "many" written accounts of Jesus studiously, and made an effort to

sift through the relevant oral traditions. Luke claims to be a thorough historian who has done his scholarly homework.

4. What is the point of Luke's effort? He writes so that Theophilus "may know the truth" concerning Jesus. The ESV translates a bit more literally, "so that you may have certainty concerning the things you have been taught" (Luke 1:4). Luke has written his Gospel, paying close attention to the sources at his disposal, so that the reader might have confidence concerning who Jesus was, what he did, and why he matters. The "why he matters" part is expanded in Luke's second volume, which we call the Acts of the Apostles.

I'll have more to say about the prologue to Luke's Gospel later. For our present purposes, I am most interested in Luke's identification of two sorts of sources for his writing: oral sources and written sources. Both of these, according to Luke, derive from eyewitnesses who were also teachers in the church.

Written Sources for the Gospels

Unfortunately, Luke did not name his written sources. Neither did the other evangelists, if indeed they also used written sources. For centuries scholars have pondered the question of Gospel sources. Classically, it was believed that Matthew was the first Gospel, and that Matthew influenced Mark and Luke. Some scholars still argue for this conclusion. The majority, however, have come to believe that the "two-source" hypothesis best explains the relationship between the Synoptic Gospels. This hypothesis is captured in the diagram on the following page.

Though I don't have the space to explain the reasons for this schema, I do want to make five quick comments.

1. "Q" is an abbreviation for *Quelle*, the German word for "source." It is a hypothetical document, invented to explain the complex relationships among the Synoptic Gospels. Q is a collection of more than 200 sayings that appear in both Matthew and Luke but not in Mark. Though a few scholars try to explain the existence of these sayings by arguing that Luke

Gospel Source Theories

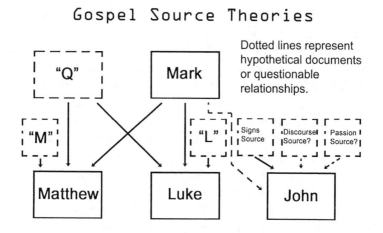

used Matthew in addition to Mark, this theory hasn't gained widespread acceptance.

2. The majority of New Testament scholars believe that Matthew used Mark as one of his major sources. Matthew's other sources included Q and "M," which is shorthand for "Matthean sources." M would contain material that is unique to Matthew, such as the visit of the Magi. There are a few scholars who argue that Matthew wrote first, and Mark abridged Matthew, but it's hard to account for the peculiarities of Matthew and Mark according to this scenario.

3. "L" is shorthand for "Lukan sources," which would include, for example, the infancy narratives in Luke. Some have suggested that L contains remembrances of Mary, Jesus' mother.

4. The Gospel of John stands apart from the Synoptic Gospels both in style and in some of its content, though similarities between John and the Synoptics abound. Some scholars have argued that John knew Mark's Gospel account and wrote to supplement it. Others have disputed this claim. Most students of John believe that he used one or more sources, especially a "Signs Source," and perhaps a source containing discourses of Jesus and a source describing Jesus' death. We can't be sure about these theories, however.

5. My guess is that reality was actually more complex than what is depicted in the chart above. L, for example, may have been several documents. Likewise with M, and perhaps even Q. Remember that Luke refers to "many" written accounts upon which he based his Gospel.

In light of Luke's prologue and the nature of the Gospels themselves, it seems likely that some framework like the one pictured above accurately reflects the sources for the Gospels. Q belongs to the same time period as Mark, given its use by Matthew and Luke. But it is impossible to date the written sources precisely, though some scholars have given it the ol' college try. Nevertheless, the fact that the evangelists used older sources increases the likelihood that what they portrayed about Jesus actually happened. Matthew, Luke, and John, and perhaps Mark, based their compositions upon older sources that were written within fifteen to thirty years of Jesus' death. They didn't just make things up from scratch.

Oral Sources for the Gospels

Nor did they use only written materials. Luke states specifically what is surely true of the other evangelists as well, that they incorporated in their writings materials that "were handed on to us by those who from the beginning were eyewitnesses and servants of the word" (Luke 1:2). These were handed on orally in the community of the early followers of Jesus.

The second-century church leader Papias, whom we have met previously in this book, described the history of the Gospel of Mark in a way that is curiously similar to Luke's prologue. Here, once again, is Papias's description:

> Mark having become the interpreter of Peter, wrote down accurately, though not in order, whatsoever he remembered of the things said or done by Christ. For he neither heard the Lord nor followed him, but afterward, as I said, he followed Peter, who adapted his teaching to the needs of his hearers, but with no intention of giving a connected account of the Lord's dis-

courses, so that Mark committed no error while he thus wrote some things as he remembered them. For he was careful of one thing, not to omit any of the things which he had heard, and not to state any of them falsely.[1]

Mark, who was not an eyewitness of Jesus, depended on sources, in this case the things he had heard Peter teach. Peter could surely be described as one who from the beginning was an eyewitness and a servant of the word, to use Luke's wording. Whether Mark used sources besides what he had learned from Peter we do not know, though it's certainly possible.

Luke was not the only New Testament writer to refer to the process of oral tradition. The verb "to hand on," a technical term for the passing on of oral tradition, appears in one of Paul's letters to the Corinthians, where he describes receiving and delivering oral traditions about Jesus:

> For I handed on to you as of first importance what I in turn had received: that Christ died for our sins in accordance with the scriptures, and that he was buried, and that he was raised on the third day in accordance with the scriptures, and that he appeared to Cephas, then to the twelve (1 Cor. 15:3–5).

Paul's testimony concerning early Christian oral tradition is significant for several reasons. Among them is the fact that he wrote his first letter to the Corinthians in the early 50s A.D., prior to the composition of the Gospels. Thus, within about twenty years of Jesus' death we have clear evidence that the early Christians were passing on information about Jesus. Moreover, the wording of the tradition Paul mentions sounds stylized, which would have facilitated the accurate transmission of that tradition. Paul was delivering to the Corinthians the exact message that had been given to him earlier. This doesn't mean that all of the early traditions about Jesus were memorized and passed on verbatim, of course, but it does suggest that this sort of thing both could and did happen, and that it was

1. Quoted in Eusebius, *Church History* 3.39.15–16.

important to the early followers of Jesus to pass on traditions about him accurately.

Following the death and resurrection of Jesus, his early followers passed on stories about him and things he said. This often happened, as Luke mentions in his prologue, in the context of the ministry of the word, namely preaching and teaching. At an early stage in this process the teachings of Jesus were translated from Aramaic, the primary language spoken by Jesus, to Greek, the dominant language of the Mediterranean world. No doubt this happened in bilingual communities, where people spoke both Aramaic and Greek, and in missionary efforts among Greek-speaking Gentiles. Not too long after Jesus' death, his teachings were being passed on mostly in a language different from the one in which he had taught, except for a few words that echoed his original Aramaic (words like *abba*, Aramaic for "father," in Mark 14:36; and *talitha cum*, Aramaic for "Little girl, get up!" in Mark 5:41).[2]

It's certainly possible that at a very early date some of the stories and sayings of Jesus were written down, but we have no evidence to prove this conjecture. The fact is that the culture in which the first disciples of Jesus lived was predominantly an oral, not a literary one. People told and remembered things more than recording them in writing. The rabbis were adept at remembering and passing on the oral Torah to their disciples, who accurately retained both the oral Torah and the commentary of their masters. But even first-century Jewish pop culture had a strong oral component. In the synagogue and around the family table, in religious gatherings and at parties, in educational settings and at wedding receptions, people told stories, quoted bits of wisdom, and in so doing shaped the culture in which they lived.

This is the culture in which early Christianity flourished, in which eyewitnesses of Jesus spoke of what they had seen, in

---

2. It is likely that Jesus was able to read Hebrew, and he may have been able to speak rudimentary Greek as well. For further discussion, see my web series, *What Language(s) Did Jesus Speak and Why Does It Matter?* http://markdroberts.com /htmfiles/resources/jesuslanguage.htm.

which communities of his followers heard, remembered, and passed on what they had been told. Thus Luke and the other evangelists found themselves with ample material for putting in writing what had mainly been passed on verbally.

But was this oral tradition reliable? Did early Christian stories about Jesus accurately portray what really happened? Did the Christian version of the teachings of Jesus reflect what he had once proclaimed? I'll address these questions in the next chapter.

Chapter 6

Did Early Christian Oral Tradition Reliably Pass Down the Truth about Jesus?

Those who discount the historical reliability of the Gospels claim that the oral tradition concerning Jesus was corrupted by human error and the hyperactive imaginations of the early Christians. To prove their point, critics sometimes roll out the example of playing "Telephone."

If you're not familiar with Telephone, which is sometimes called "Whisper Down the Alley," let me explain. First, you get a bunch of people to sit in a circle. Then somebody starts by secretly writing down a sentence. Usually it's something like: "Pastor Mark is going to the fair tomorrow because he's meeting a friend there." After writing down the sentence, the writer whispers it to the next person in the circle. Then that person turns to the next person and whispers the message. So it goes, all the way around the circle. When the message comes to the last person, that one says out loud what he or she thinks is the right message. Then the person who started the communication reads the original message for all to hear. Inevitably, the final sentence is quite different from the original. "Pastor Mark is going to the fair tomorrow because he's meeting a friend there" has become "Pastor Mark is going to float up into the air tomorrow because he's so full of hot air."

Does the game of Telephone prove that the oral tradition about Jesus cannot be trusted? No. In fact, the limitations of the Telephone analogy will help us understand why we *can* put trust in the oral traditions about Jesus that are found in the Gospels.

The Context of the Oral Tradition about Jesus

The game of Telephone works because we aren't adept at memorizing. Let's face it. We don't memorize very well because we don't have to. Consider the case of phone numbers. When I was young, I had memorized at least twenty-five phone numbers. I could call my friends, my grandparents, the local movie theater . . . all from memory. But along came memory chips and phones that "remember" frequently called numbers. Now I may have less then ten phone numbers in my brain. Even some that I call most frequently, like my wife's cell phone, I don't know by heart.

Yet people can be trained to memorize, even in today's visual, electronic culture. When my wife was training to be a marriage and family counselor, she was expected to write out "verbatims" of her sessions with clients. Verbatims were accurate, in-depth transcripts of what was discussed over the course of an hour. In time, Linda became quite proficient at this. Why? It was a matter of necessity and practice. Her professional context required and supported it.

The early followers of Jesus lived in an oral culture. Relatively few people were literate. Only the wealthy had access to libraries and literature. So people needed good memories. They remembered stories, sayings, Scripture passages, and you name it (well, not phone numbers!). Their oral culture had contexts in which crucial information, like religious stories, would be passed on faithfully. Teachers and storytellers were expected to hand on what they had been told accurately, though with a modicum of freedom. Since they did their work in community gatherings, if they got the story substantially wrong, the community in which they functioned would hold them accountable for their mistake.[1]

I don't know if anybody has ever tried playing Telephone with people from an oral culture. My guess is this game wouldn't be much fun among such people because they would pass on the message accurately. Yet when it comes to the oral tradition about Jesus, we have much more than merely the cultural context to assure its accurate transmission.

The People of the Oral Tradition about Jesus

As I've already mentioned, the Telephone game works, in part, because the players aren't adept at memorization. Those who passed on the traditions about Jesus were, on the contrary, trained by culture to memorize and recount with considerable accuracy. Moreover, if Birger Gerhardsson's connection of early Christianity with Jewish rabbinic traditions holds any water, then some of those who passed on the sayings of Jesus had been specifically trained to do this with exemplary precision.[2]

1. For information on oral culture in general and its relevance to the Gospels, see: Kenneth E. Bailey, "Controlled Oral Tradition and the Synoptic Gospels," *Themelios* 20/2 (January 1995): 4–11 (http://www.biblicalstudies.org.uk/article_tradition_bailey. html); Kenneth E. Bailey, *Poet and Peasant and Through Peasant Eyes*, combined ed. (Grand Rapids, Mich.: Eerdmans, 1983); Birger Gerhardsson, *The Reliability of the Gospel Tradition* (Peabody, Mass: Hendrickson, 2001); Alfred B. Lord, *The Singer of Tales*, 2nd paperback ed. (Cambridge, Mass.: Harvard University Press, 2000); N. T. Wright, *The New Testament and the People of God* (Minneapolis: Augsburg/Fortress, 1996), 418–443.

2. Gerhardsson, *Reliability of the Gospel Tradition*.

No doubt lots of average Christians told stories about Jesus in the years before the Gospels were written. They passed these accounts on to their friends and children. But this doesn't mean that just anybody could tell and retell these stories in the gathered Christian community. Don't forget Luke's claim that he had received the traditions from "those who from the beginning were eyewitnesses and servants of the word" (Luke 1:2). He's referring here to the people we call the apostles, in particular the apostles who had been with Jesus during his earthly ministry. These eyewitnesses, who had been set apart by Jesus himself, were the official "players" in the Jesus Telephone game.

On top of this, we must remember who started up the early Christian game of Telephone: Jesus himself. He was the first player, if you will, the one who first spoke the message to be passed along. And he wasn't just any old player, at least in the eyes of his followers. They thought he was the Messiah, the Savior of Israel, and the One through whom God was inaugurating his kingdom. They saw Jesus not only as a wise teacher but also, in some way, as the very embodiment of God's Wisdom. And, in what was shocking to the majority of Jews in the first century, the earliest Christians confessed Jesus to be Lord: not just an authoritative human being, but somehow God in human form. Thus they had lots of motivation to remember what he said and to transmit it accurately. They weren't just playing games at a party.

The Content of the Oral Tradition about Jesus

The early Christians also thought that Jesus' teaching was uniquely true and more important than any other ideas in the world. Consider, for example, the following passages from the Gospels:

> "Everyone then who hears these words of mine and acts on them will be like a wise man who built his house on rock" (Matt. 7:24).

"Heaven and earth will pass away, but my words will not pass away" (Mark 13:31).

"It is the spirit that gives life; the flesh is useless. The words that I have spoken to you are spirit and life" (John 6:63).

So Jesus asked the twelve, "Do you also wish to go away?" Simon Peter answered him, "Lord, to whom can we go? You have the words of eternal life" (John 6:67–68).

"If you abide in me, and my words abide in you, ask for whatever you wish, and it will be done for you" (John 15:7).

The early Christians believed all these things to be true about Jesus' words. Thus they had every reason to pass on the sayings of Jesus accurately. The same would go for accounts of his actions, by the way.

Moreover, the forms in which the sayings and deeds of Jesus were transmitted contributed to the precision of the transmission. One of the reasons the Telephone game works is that the sentence being passed around the circle is usually odd and hard to repeat verbatim. If the originator of the process were to write a short poem, with obvious meter and rhyme, and if that poem made sense, then odds are much higher that it would be passed around correctly.

Many of the sayings of Jesus facilitate memorization. Some involve striking images that you won't soon forget: "It is easier for a camel to go through the eye of a needle than for someone who is rich to enter the kingdom of God" (Mark 10:25). Others use few words to make the point: "You cannot serve God and wealth" (Matt. 6:24). Still others use parallelism of some kind (for example, the house built on the sand versus the house built on the rock, Matt. 7:24–27). Of course many of Jesus' key teachings come in the form of parables, short stories that leave a strong impression on the mind.

In the last century, New Testament scholars studied the oral forms in which the traditions about Jesus were passed along before they were written down. Many of the first "form critics," like Rudolf Bultmann, combined form criticism with a high degree of skepticism about the historicity of the Gospels— unnecessarily, I might add. In fact, the formal nature of oral tradition contributes to memorization and faithful transmission. If, for example, you're trying to learn the Beatitudes in Matthew 5, think of how much it helps that each line has the form: "Blessed are (they) . . . for theirs (they) . . ."

The oral forms of the Jesus tradition also ensured the truthful passing down of stories about him. Consider the example of the miracle stories in the Gospels. They almost always include the following elements: a statement of the problem; the brief description of the miracle; a statement of the response. This makes logical sense, of course, but it also conditions the mind to remember and relate miracle stories faithfully. It's rather like how jokes can take on a familiar form, thus helping us to remember them: "A priest, a minister, and a rabbi . . ." or "Knock, knock . . ."

The Community of the Oral Tradition about Jesus

My favorite high school teacher was Mr. Bottaro. He was my English teacher in tenth grade, and I was blessed to have him in twelfth grade as well. Mr. Bottaro was energetic, incisive, and passionate. I can still remember his ardent reading of Dylan Thomas's poem, "Do Not Go Gentle into That Good Night," as he tried to get fifteen-year-old kids to think about their mortality. Mr. Bottaro was always talking about death and how taking it seriously helped us to live to the fullest.

One day during the spring of my senior year, my fellow students and I arrived in Mr. Bottaro's class, but he wasn't there. When the bell rang, we were still without a teacher. Then, about five minutes later, the school principal showed up. He informed us that Mr. Bottaro had died in his sleep the night before. We sat in stunned silence. Many students began to weep. It was one of the saddest days of my life.

During the days that followed, we reminisced plenty about Mr. Bottaro, in class, during the lunch hour, and after his memorial service. Apart from being a fine teacher, he was a character, and an eminently quotable one at that. In the telling of stories we shared our common grief over our loss and our common joy over having had such a wonderful teacher.

In those days of storytelling, the community of Mr. Bottaro's students reinforced our corporate memory. By agreeing together about what our teacher had done and said, we celebrated his life and we fixed certain events and sayings in our minds. If, during that time, somebody had told a story about Mr. Bottaro that contradicted our common memory—if, for example, someone had accused him of playing favorites or of *disliking* "Do Not Go Gentle into That Good Night," then we would have surely set that person right. Our community ensured the basic truthfulness of oral traditions about our beloved teacher.

And so it was with the community of Jesus in the first years after his death. Not only were there recognized leaders, those who had walked with Jesus and been inundated with his teachings, but also the whole community acted together to provide a place for the telling of stories about Jesus and for weighing those stories by community memory.

Sometimes you'll hear skeptics talk about the oral period before the writing of the Gospels as if it were a free-for-all, a time when anybody could be inspired by the Spirit to put all sorts of words into Jesus' mouth. But there is little evidence that this sort of thing actually happened, and plenty of evidence that it did not happen. After all, the early Christians believed Jesus was uniquely special as a teacher, and they believed his words were both authoritative and life-giving. Thus they had strong motivation to remember and accurately pass on what he had said, even when it was translated from Aramaic into Greek. The early Christian community helped to make sure this happened effectively. Here's what Birger Gerhardsson concludes about the purported creativity of the oral tradition about Jesus:

My contention is thus that we have every reason to proceed on the assumption that Jesus' closest disciples had an authoritative position in early Christianity as witnesses and bearers of the traditions of what Jesus had said and done. There is no reason to suppose that any believer in the early church could create traditions about Jesus and expect that his word would be accepted.[3]

Gerhardsson's observation is confirmed by the fact that so much in the oral tradition about Jesus does not reflect the needs of the early church. At some points it even appears to contradict those needs. If Christians were making up sayings of Jesus willy-nilly, and if these were being accepted uncritically by the church, then we should expect to have much more helpful instruction from Jesus concerning such contentious issues as Jewish-Christian relationships, the Sabbath, women in ministry, apostolic authority, and even his own messiahship. But this is not what we have in the Gospels. In fact, the community of Jesus' followers carefully conserved what he had said, making sure the process of oral tradition was faithful to what Jesus really said and didn't say.

The Process of the Oral Tradition about Jesus

The Telephone game assumes that the communication of the key sentence will be done secretly, with players whispering to each other.

Think of what would happen in Telephone if somebody changed the rules. Rather than whispering the sentence, the first player says it out loud to the person next in line. This person says the same sentence out loud to the next person, and so forth and so on. This would be a boring game, to say the least, because all players would hear what was being passed around.

That's more or less what happened in the early Christian community when it came to passing down the teaching of Jesus. It was not done secretly, but openly. Remember that Luke got

3. Ibid., 39.

his information from eyewitnesses who were also "servants of the word" (Luke 1:2). They were teaching about Jesus in the public square and in the church. Their stories about Jesus and their accounts of his sayings were part of the public record, if you will, or at least the public church record.

When you think of how little material actually appears in the Gospels compared with all that Jesus would have done and said, it's obvious that the "servants of the word" tended to repeat themselves a lot. The same stories about Jesus were told and retold. Given the variation we see in the Gospels, these stories and sayings weren't delivered in exactly the same words every time. This would be especially true when the original Aramaic of Jesus was translated into Greek. Nevertheless, the members of the earliest churches would have heard the same stories and sayings again and again in much the same way they were first told by the eyewitnesses.

Repetition facilitates memory, even precise memory. I can say the Lord's Prayer, the 23rd Psalm, the Pledge of Allegiance, and even my VISA card number because I have repeated them so often. I can sing more than a hundred hymns and songs, not because I'm so musical but because I'm in four worship services every weekend and I rarely miss church! The early Christians came to know a core of Jesus' sayings and stories about him because they heard them and repeated them so frequently.

Curiously enough, there was one tradition in early Christianity that prized itself on having secret teachings from Jesus, ones that were not widely known among most Christians. This was a core feature of Christian Gnosticism. When orthodox Christians objected that Gnostic theology didn't come from Jesus, the Gnostics claimed that the divine Christ had revealed secret information to a few select disciples. They were the only ones privy to the secret, and they passed it on only to the few elites who could receive the revelation. But this essential element of Gnostic tradition, its secrecy, counts strongly against the possibility that it truly represents the teachings of Jesus.

Closing Thoughts

When my daughter, Kara, was four years old, I decided to teach her the Lord's Prayer. Did I simplify the language so she might understand it? Of course not. I wanted my daughter to learn the "real words" of the Lord's Prayer. So I taught Kara the old-fashioned words that my parents had once taught me (except I used my Presbyterian "debts" instead of their Methodist "trespasses").

Kara didn't understand what many of the words meant. Fancy that! But she tried her best to imitate my sounds. Some of her efforts were delightful. When I said, "Our Father who art in heaven, hallowed be thy name," she said, "Our Father who art in heaven, Hollywood be my name." Or when I prayed, "Forgive us our debts as we forgive our debtors," she said, "Forgive us our dents, as we forgive our dentist." How logical! Yet because I cared that Kara learn the real words, I gently corrected her and helped her get both the sounds and the meaning right. Today, my eleven-year-old daughter says the Lord's Prayer flawlessly. I expect that someday she'll pass it on to *her* children.

Similarly, the early Christians, and especially the teachers, made sure that the words of Jesus were carefully though not slavishly preserved. They had their transitions from "trespasses" to "debts," or from the Aramaic *abba* to the Greek *pater*. But the community made sure that innovations like "Hollywood be my name" never made it into the authoritative tradition! Rather, they remembered what Jesus said and made sure this was passed down accurately.

The idea of early Christians memorizing substantial traditions about Jesus may seem unrealistic, even given what I've said about the context, people, content, community, and process of the oral tradition about Jesus. But consider the following contemporary analogy.

All Muslims are expected to memorize portions of the Qur'an. But many go on to memorize the entire book, which contains more than 80,000 Arabic words. The one who does this is called a *Hafiz* and is highly regarded among other Muslims. Muslims claim that millions of the faithful have achieved this status, even today.

What enables a Muslim to memorize the entire Qur'an? Context helps, in that even though most Muslims can read, their religious life is inundated by the recitation of the Qur'an. This repetition is reinforced by the poetic nature of the Qur'an itself, and by the way it is chanted. Of course the respect given to the *Hafiz* encourages Muslims who are trying to memorize the whole book. But the greatest motivation of all for a pious Muslim is the belief that the Qur'an contains Allah's own words. To memorize the Qur'an is to internalize the very words of God.

In a similar vein, the early followers of Jesus had both the ability and the motivation to pass on oral tradition with accuracy. The combination of context, people, content, community, and process helped them to faithfully recount what Jesus did and said. A study of the Gospels shows that the early Christians did this very thing with considerable success. Thus the first-century dating of Matthew, Mark, Luke, and John, combined with their use of earlier oral traditions, combined with early Christian faithfulness in passing on these oral traditions, add up to a convincing rationale for trusting the Gospels. What we find in these books accurately represents what Jesus himself actually did and said. We may not have the original Aramaic words of Jesus, except in a few cases, and we may not have the first Aramaic stories about him, but we have Greek translations that faithfully reproduce Jesus' actual words and deeds.

Chapter 7

What Are the New Testament Gospels?

What are the New Testament Gospels? Are they histories? Biographies? Novels? Or . . . ? To which genre should they be assigned? And why does this matter when we're considering the trustworthiness of the Gospels?

To answer the last question first, if we know the genre of the Gospels, this will help us interpret them appropriately. If it turns out, for example, that the Gospels are short novels, then we ought not to fret too much about their historicity. If they are biographies or histories, however, then we would be wise to evaluate them as to whether they are valid sources of information about their main character, Jesus of Nazareth.

One of the greatest problems when it comes to the genre of the Gospels is the natural tendency to compare them to contemporary examples. This problem manifests itself in a variety of ways. For example, if we think of the Gospels in terms of modern biographies, then they are woefully inadequate. They lack much of what we have come to expect in a biography:

background on the person's family; insight into contemporary social events; stories of the person's childhood; and so forth and so on. Plus, the Gospels are way too short. So, if we're thinking in modern terms, then the Gospels are not biographies, or else they're poor ones.[1]

And yet they are biographical in a sense. They focus on one person. They narrate events from his life. They include some of his sayings. They have much to say, relatively speaking, about his death. We expect such things from biographies.

We're in a similar quandary if we think of the Gospels in terms of modern historical writing. They are far too short to be displayed in the "History" section of your local bookstore. This is true in comparison not only to recent historiography but also to classics of ancient history. The Gospels are not nearly as long as the histories of Herodotus and Thucydides, or the first-century Jewish historian Josephus. So it would seem strange to label the Gospels as histories.

And yet they seem to be historical in a sense. They purport to relate what happened in a certain period of time. They connect those events to important personages, like King Herod or Pontius Pilate. Luke, in particular, looks rather like some sort of history. I have previously mentioned how much the prologue to the third Gospel resembles the sort of thing we would find in the history writing of Luke's day. Moreover, the third Gospel is the first part of a longer work that includes Acts. Luke/Acts has the kind of breadth we associate with a work of history.

The Gospels as Hellenistic Biographies

Not long ago it was common for New Testament scholars to give up trying to fit the Gospels into existing genres, such as biography or history. The Gospels are unique, it was claimed. No other kind of literature narrates a small number of stories

---

1. For a wise and readable discussion of the genre of the Gospels, see the "Prolegomenon" to Ben Witherington III, *New Testament History: A Narrative Account* (Grand Rapids, Mich.: Baker, 2001), 14–28.

and sayings of a particular individual and then spends a dispro-
portionate amount of space describing his death. What is the
genre of the Gospels? They are Gospels, plain and simple.

This was the party line when I began my academic studies
in New Testament. The Gospels were said to be like ancient
biographies, histories, romances, and "aretologies" (accounts
of a famous person's great deeds). But, given their peculiar
form and their focus on the death of Jesus, the Gospels were
said to be a unique genre. There is still a measure of truth in
this perspective, because the biblical Gospels are unique in
some ways. And, I might add, they are quite different in form
from the noncanonical so-called Gospels, few of which relate
stories of Jesus' life or focus on his death. Nevertheless, recent
scholarship on the New Testament Gospels has tended to recognize how much they are a kind of biography, not modern
biography so much as Hellenistic biography.[2]

By and large, Greco-Roman biographies were not the mammoth tomes we find in our bookstores today but shorter and
more focused works. It was common for a biography to skip
over major parts of a character's life, limiting discussion to
key events or speeches. These deeds and words were chosen
and organized, not out of antiquarian curiosity but rather to
make a moral statement for the readers. The subject of the
biography exemplified certain virtues. Emphasizing these encouraged readers to emulate the virtuous life of the biographical subject.

When seen in this light, the New Testament Gospels fit quite
nicely within the genre of Hellenistic biography. The Gospels
are distinctive in some ways, including their theological emphases and their focus on the death of Jesus, but they fit the
general category of Hellenistic biography.

Luke is unique among the Gospels in having a companion
volume that narrates the events of the early church. If one thinks

---

2. This case has been presented persuasively by Richard A. Burridge in his book,
What Are the Gospels? A Comparison with Graeco-Roman Biography (Grand Rapids,
Mich.: Eerdmans, 2004). For a shorter version of this argument, see Witherington,
New Testament History, 19–24.

of Luke/Acts together, biography isn't the most appropriate genre, although Acts focuses mainly on the activities of Peter and Paul and thus has biographical touches. It would be better to see Luke/Acts as fitting within the genre of Hellenistic history. In fact, it also bears resemblance to the Old Testament histories (1 and 2 Samuel, etc.), which focus primarily on major individuals as they unfold the story of God's saving work in the world.

Hellenistic biography and history share in common an ordered narrative of the past. Yet these were not academic treatises. Writings in these genres sought primarily to derive moral lessons from the people and events of the past. They were written to teach, to exhort, and to improve their readers.

The Literary Freedom of the Hellenistic Biographer or Historian

Those who do not believe that the New Testament Gospels provide reliable historical information about Jesus often point to variations in the wording of sayings as they appear in different Gospels, to differences in the order of events between the Gospels, or other characteristics that seem inconsistent with the genres of biography and history. For example, when Jesus is baptized by John in the Jordan River, a voice from heaven speaks, but the words differ slightly between Matthew and Mark (Luke agrees with Mark):

> And a voice from heaven said, "This is my Son, the Beloved, with whom I am well pleased" (Matt. 3:17).

> And a voice came from heaven, "You are my Son, the Beloved; with you I am well pleased" (Mark 1:11).

This sort of difference delights detractors of the Gospels and perplexes the faithful. It would be pretty hard to argue that the voice from heaven said the same sentence twice in slightly different ways (though I expect this argument has been made somewhere). No, it seems more likely that Matthew and Mark used slightly different words for the same vocal event. If Matthew was using Mark, as is likely, then he made a few changes. How could he do this if he is writing biography or history? Do the differences between Matthew and Mark prove that one of the Gospels is wrong? Does this mean that either Matthew or Mark was a sloppy historian?

If we evaluate the evangelists in light of contemporary history writing, then we would have to say that one of them doesn't measure up. We expect historians and biographers to quote their sources with precision. For example, my friend Ronald C. White, Jr., wrote a highly acclaimed study of Abraham Lincoln's second Inaugural, *Lincoln's Greatest Speech*.[3] If Ron had misquoted Lincoln's words, or paraphrased them and put them in quotation marks, he would have been blasted by critics. In fact, his book would never have been published in such a form.

Yet in the ancient world, before there were transcripts, tape recordings, and podcasts, biographers and historians exercised greater freedom in paraphrasing or slightly altering spoken words for stylistic reasons. A good historian, if he knew that a character had made a speech at a certain time, would get available information about that speech and then write the speech with his own words as if these words had been uttered by the character. Nowadays, a historian who did this would be considered sloppy at best, or even dishonest. (Remember the case of Jayson Blair, not a historian, but a reporter for the *New York Times*. He disgraced the *Times* and himself by, among other things, making up quotes that his sources could have said but didn't in fact say.)

So, assuming for a moment that Matthew used Mark as a source, if we evaluate Matthew according to today's standards, then we would say he's not completely reliable, even though he mostly agrees with Mark. Yet this sort of anachronistic

---

3. Ronald C. White, Jr., *Lincoln's Greatest Speech* (New York: Simon & Schuster, 2002).

approach is unhelpful, not to mention unfair to Matthew. For reasons of style or story, Matthew was doing what historians and biographers in his day were expected to do. Nobody would have accused him of falsehood back then. Nor should we.

The proof of this is obvious and, I think, incontrovertible. Both Matthew and Mark were accepted as authoritative in the early church, even though the sayings of Jesus are usually worded differently in Matthew and Mark. The events of the Gospels don't always come in exactly the same order, either. The early Christians didn't see these variations as a problem because that's what they were accustomed to in their biographical and historical writings.

It sometimes comes as a shock when Christians discover that the Gospels don't present the sayings of Jesus in exactly the same way, or don't give the same details when telling what must obviously be the same story. Skeptics love this sort of thing and use it to diminish confidence in the Gospels. But both scandalized Christians and zealous skeptics must learn to see the Gospels in the context of their own time and history.

Moreover, we must remember that the Gospels give us what is technically called the *ipsissima vox* ("his own voice") of Jesus rather than the *ipsissima verba* ("his own words"). Since it's highly unlikely that Jesus did much teaching in Greek, the autographs of Matthew, Mark, Luke, and John did not preserve his original words (except in a few cases). They do, however, authentically capture his voice.

"All Truth Is God's Truth"

When I was a freshman in college and was struggling with my first New Testament class, I wondered if faith and reason simply didn't fit together. I feared that if I wanted to be a confident Christian, I would have to avoid thinking carefully and critically about my faith, especially the Bible. Discovering the variations among the Gospels unsettled my confidence in their reliability. I couldn't deny the facts of these differences among the Gospels; but I couldn't figure out how to reconcile them with what I had previously believed about their trustworthiness. For this reason, and others like it, I entered an extended season of doubting the veracity of the Gospels. I described this in more detail in chapter 1.

In the midst of my intellectual turmoil, John R. W. Stott visited the Harvard campus. A highly respected Christian thinker and expert in the New Testament, Dr. Stott attended an informal dessert gathering hosted by a friend of mine. *Here was my chance to talk with someone who might understand my dilemma*, I thought. *Maybe I can get some help from him.*

When another student finished a conversation, I seized my chance. "Dr. Stott," I said, "I'm taking a New Testament class. Much of what I'm being taught contradicts what I believe about the Bible. I'm beginning to wonder if it's unwise to study Scripture in an academic way. I'd like to take more classes in New Testament, yet I'm afraid that what I learn will undermine my faith. What should I do?"

"I can understand your conflict and your fear," Dr. Stott began, "because I've felt them myself. Many of the popular theories in New Testament scholarship do challenge orthodox Christianity."

"But," he continued, "you don't have to be afraid. Let me tell you something that will give you confidence as you study: *All truth is God's truth.* There isn't anything true about the Bible that God doesn't already know. You don't have to fear that if you dig too deeply you'll undermine genuine Christian faith. You may indeed discover that some of your beliefs aren't correct. In fact, I hope you do make this discovery, many times over. That's what happens when you live under biblical authority. But you never have to be afraid of seeking the genuine truth because all truth is God's truth."

This was a watershed moment in my life. On the one hand, it pointed me in the direction of biblical scholarship, a path I have followed for the last thirty years and which has enabled me to write this book. On the other hand, though Dr. Stott didn't have time to deal with my specific struggles, the fact that he knew what I was going through and had managed to maintain a solid faith in biblical authority encouraged me to keep on seeking the truth about the Bible.

I expect that some readers of my book will be unsettled by part of what I'm saying about the Gospels. So far I've questioned whether or not John wrote the fourth Gospel and I've noted that Matthew and Mark use slightly different words for God's proclamation when Jesus was baptized. This may be unsettling for some folks, maybe even for you. My encouragement is to keep on pressing for what is true. Don't take my word for it. Don't settle for believing things about the Gospels that are not true. And don't fear that some undiscovered truth out there will overturn your trust in the Gospels. John Stott was right: "There isn't anything true about the Bible that God doesn't already know." Indeed, "all truth *is* God's truth."

Before I leave this story, I want to make another point. I have told you about my encounter with Dr. Stott to the very best of my memory. I'm quite sure that I have the main facts correct. It was Dr. Stott with whom I spoke, not C. S. Lewis. The conversation did happen during the spring semester of my freshman year. And Dr. Stott did encourage me to keep on looking for truth. I'm almost positive he said, "All truth is God's truth." (I found out later that Dr. Stott was quoting from the Christian theologian St. Augustine.) But I don't have a tape recording of that conversation. And I didn't rush back to my dorm to write down exactly what Dr. Stott had said. In telling this story, I have made up words and put them in Dr. Stott's mouth. Though I'm confident I have his *ipsissima vox*, I don't have his *ipsissima verba*, except for "All truth is God's truth." Moreover, I've told this story before in print—in my book *Dare to Be True*—using slightly different words.[4] Therefore, what I've done in telling this story is similar in many ways to what Hellenistic historians and biographers—including the evangelists—used to do.

4. Mark D. Roberts, *Dare to Be True* (Colorado Springs: WaterBrook, 2003), 24–25.

Does my admission surprise you? I doubt it. Though you may not have considered this as you read, I expect you sensed that I was telling the story from memory, using my own words, even as I "quoted" Dr. Stott. You knew from the kind of narrative I was offering that I was not using a tape or transcript. Moreover, now that you have my confession, do you doubt the truthfulness of my story? I doubt this too. You probably believe that, though I may not have gotten every jot and tittle absolutely right, I have related my conversation with Dr. Stott in a trustworthy manner. (At least I hope you believe this! And if you don't believe that I'm usually a truthful person, you probably shouldn't bother reading this book!)

Is it possible to trust a biographical or historical writing that offers the *ipsissima vox* rather than the *ipsissima verba*? I believe it is. Of course this depends on your evaluation of the overall trustworthiness of the writer and the sources at his or her disposal. I've already talked about the sources used by the evangelists and how they contribute to the historicity of the Gospels. I'll have much more to say about their general trustworthiness in the rest of this book.

The Genre of the Gospels and Their Reliability

I know I've covered a lot of ground in a short time, but let me wrap up this chapter with a few conclusions.

1. The Gospels are best understood as Hellenistic biographies with several characteristics that reflect the uniqueness of their subject matter and purpose. Luke straddles the fence of biography and history.

2. The Gospel writers functioned in the mode of the biography and history writers of their day. This means they were permitted greater freedom in certain matters than would be granted to modern biographers and historians. Paraphrasing or rephrasing statements and speeches was acceptable, as was arranging events in thematic rather than chronological order.

3. When we evaluate the New Testament Gospels in their own literary and cultural context, we can understand how reliable they are and the ways in which they are reliable. For example, the Gospels can faithfully represent the *ipsissima vox* of Jesus without reproducing his *ipsissima verba*. Minor variations of wording or a different ordering of events do not mean that we should discount the reliability of the Gospels as sources of genuine knowledge of Jesus. They do mean that we must closely examine the intent and process of the Gospel writers, however, in order not to misconstrue their purposes.

4. Naysayers who deride the reliability of the Gospels because of such things as verbal inconsistencies between the Gospels are making an error of anachronism. Their negativity is almost as silly as criticizing the Gospels for failing to include digital photographs of Jesus.

My mentioning the inconsistencies between the Gospels raises the question of how the existence of four biblical Gospels impacts our evaluation of their reliability. To this topic we'll turn in the next chapter.

Chapter 8

What Difference Does It Make That There Are Four Gospels?

Around A.D. 175, a Syrian Christian named Tatian produced a comprehensive harmony of Matthew, Mark, Luke, and John called the *Diatessaron*. It included almost all of the four Gospels, with strands carefully woven together into a seamless narrative of the ministry of Jesus. The Greek word *diatessaron* means "through four." Tatian had created one Gospel harmony "through four" originals. In his work of harmonization, he "cleaned up" the narrative that had been given to him in the New Testament Gospels, harmonizing apparent discrepancies, eliminating redundancies, and so forth.

For many years Tatian's harmony was the standard version of the story of Jesus in parts of the Roman empire, especially in Syria. But even there the *Diatessaron* was eventually replaced by the canonical four Gospels, which elsewhere in the early church had always been authoritative in their separate versions. The church preferred the four distinct voices of Matthew, Mark, Luke, and John, even if this distinctiveness sometimes seemed discordant. Though you would think the church might have liked the neatness and simplicity of a single, sanitized story of Jesus, in fact it hung on to the original stories in all of their peculiar richness and messiness.

So, today, we have four separate Gospels in the New Testament rather than one harmonized account of Jesus. What difference does this make in the discussion of the reliability of these Gospels?

The Benefit of Multiple Witnesses

On the most obvious level, the fact that we have four early witnesses to the ministry of Jesus increases our confidence that we can know what Jesus actually did and said. This is a matter of common sense.

Several years ago I served on a jury in a criminal case. The defendant was accused of possessing controlled substances (illegal drugs, including cocaine). Not surprisingly, he claimed that he was innocent, that the drugs found in his car were not his, and that he had no idea how they got there. But the prosecution presented several witnesses to contradict this man's story. One of the police officers who arrested him explained how he saw the defendant scurry to hide the drugs when pulled over for a traffic violation. Others bore witness to his having full awareness of the drugs in his possession.

When it came time for the jury to deliberate, we reviewed the evidence that had been presented to us. The fact that multiple witnesses testified to the defendant's guilt was persuasive. Without too much effort, we found him guilty as charged.

If we want to know something about Jesus, we're better off with four Gospels than if we had only one. And we're better off having the distinct perspectives of the evangelists rather than one blended *Diatessaron*, even if this gets untidy sometimes.

Our situation in trying to find out about Jesus from multiple sources is similar to that of scholars trying to discover something about the real Socrates. The famous fifth-century Greek philosopher didn't write anything down, or at least none of his writings have survived. Almost everything we know about Socrates comes from three writers: Plato, Xenophon, and Aristophanes. The first two were disciples of Socrates who, after the death of their master, wrote dialogues in which Socrates played a major role. Aristophanes was a comic playwright who, in his drama *The Clouds*, made Socrates out to be a buffoon. Most scholars consider Plato and Xenophon to be more reliable sources than Aristophanes for information about the historical Socrates, though their tendency to idolize their master may be balanced by Aristophanes' more critical albeit exaggerated picture. Nevertheless, the existence of three perspectives on the life of Socrates allows scholars to determine with greater confidence what he was really like and what he really taught.

In the case of Jesus, we have four different portraits, a situation that puts us in a better position than those who are seeking the real Socrates. Yet we do not have a contrary picture, like that of Aristophanes. To our knowledge, no writer in the first century wrote a satire of Jesus. We have to wait until the second century for open criticism of Jesus. The most famous of these critics was Celsus, who said of Jesus that he "invented his birth from a virgin." Celsus accused Jesus of being

born in a certain Jewish village, of a poor woman of the country, who gained her subsistence by spinning, and who was turned out of doors by her husband, a carpenter by trade, because she was convicted of adultery; that after being driven away by her husband, and wandering about for a time, she disgracefully gave birth to Jesus, an illegitimate child, who having hired himself out as a servant in Egypt on account of his poverty, and having there acquired some miraculous powers, on which the Egyptians greatly pride themselves, returned to his own country, highly

95

elated on account of them, and by means of these proclaimed himself a God.[1]

Note: it would be unwise to consider Celsus a reliable, independent witness to Jesus. In chapter 12 I'll examine in much greater detail the evidence for Jesus outside of the New Testament Gospels.

Similarities and Differences among the Four Gospels

In my first New Testament class in college, I learned about a relatively new scholarly discipline called redaction criticism (from the German term *Redaktionsgeschichte*, meaning "the history of editing" of the Gospels). Redaction critics, assuming that Matthew and Luke used Mark and Q as sources, studied the editorial changes made by Matthew and Luke. These changes revealed the distinctive theologies of their Gospels. I say "distinctive." What I heard in class, however, was "distinctive and contradictory." In that religion class, and throughout my graduate studies in New Testament, it was popular to emphasize the unique perspectives of Matthew, Mark, Luke, and John, and to minimize what they had in common, or even to deny that they had much in common at all. I heard plenty about the "contradictions" between the Gospels as my professors engaged in redaction criticism.

Some conservative scholars reacted negatively to redaction criticism, even suggesting that the discipline itself was inconsistent with biblical authority. But most evangelical scholars have come to see both the good and the bad in redaction criticism. The good has been identifying the distinctive efforts of the Gospel writers, who didn't merely collect material and paste it together, but who carefully wove that material into a coherent and creative narrative. Redaction criticism has raised the

---

1. Celsus is quoted in Origen, *Against Celsus* 1.28. The translation is from Alexander Roberts and James Donaldson, eds., *The Ante-Nicene Fathers*, reprint ed. (Grand Rapids, Mich.: Eerdmans, 1978–1980).

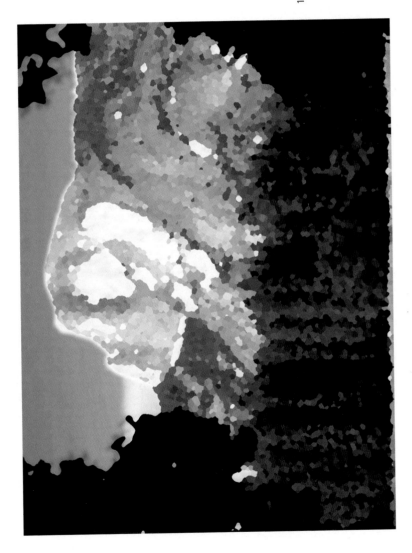

1. Half Dome,
First View

2. Half Dome,
Second View

3. Half Dome,
Third View

4. Half Dome,
Fourth View

5. The Synagogue in Capernaum

6. The Pilate Inscription

8. The Cliff at El Kursi

respect given to Matthew, Mark, Luke, and John as creative, careful writers, and not mere collectors of traditions.

The bad part of redaction criticism has been the tendency of many who use this methodology to exaggerate the differences among the Gospels. Nobody doubts that there are such differences and that they are significant. But sometimes in focusing so much on the different trees one loses sight of the common forest. Think for a moment. If you were to sit down and read Mark, and then Matthew, do you think you would come away thinking, *Now there are two unique, virtually incompatible pictures of Jesus?* Hardly! In fact, I think you would be more inclined to say, after reading Matthew, *Well, he adds some more fascinating material (like the visit of the Magi or the Sermon on the Mount) but that's mostly the same story as I found in Mark. It was rather redundant in parts, actually.*

Now I freely grant that there are significant differences among the four biblical Gospels on a number of key topics. For example, Matthew alone tells the story of the Magi's visit to the child Jesus, while Luke alone has shepherds abiding in the fields keeping watch over their flock by night. John is the most different of all, narrating the ministry of Jesus with a chronology that is more complex than what we find in the Synoptics, and adding extended discourses that are distinctive in both form and content.

Features Common to All Four Gospels

I'll have more to say about the differences among the Gospels later in this book. For now I want to focus on something that is often overlooked by scholars but is generally acknowledged by careful readers who have lots of common sense: the striking similarities between the pictures of Jesus found in the New Testament Gospels.

Here is a list of some of the details about Jesus' life and ministry that are found in *all four Gospels*—yes, including John:

97

- Jesus was a Jewish man.
- Jesus ministered during the time when Pontius Pilate was prefect of Judea (around 27 to 37 A.D.).
- Jesus had a close connection with John the Baptist, and his ministry superseded that of John.
- John the Baptist was involved with the descent of the Spirit on Jesus.
- Jesus' ministry took place in Galilee, especially his early ministry.
- Jesus' ministry concluded in Jerusalem.
- Jesus gathered disciples around him. (This is important: Jewish teachers in the time of Jesus didn't recruit their own students; rather, the students came to them.)
- The brothers Andrew and Simon (Peter) were among Jesus' first disciples.
- The followers of Jesus referred to him as "rabbi."
- Jesus taught women, and they were included among the larger group of his followers. (This, by the way, sets Jesus apart from other Jewish teachers of his day.)
- Jesus taught in Jewish synagogues.
- Jesus was popular with the masses.
- At times, however, Jesus left the crowds to be alone.
- Jesus proclaimed the "kingdom of God" (in Matthew, more commonly the "kingdom of heaven").
- Jesus called people to believe in God and in God's saving activity.
- The ministry of Jesus involved conflict with supernatural evil powers, including Satan and demons.
- Jesus used the cryptic title "Son of Man" in reference to himself and in order to explain his mission. (Jesus' fondness for and use of this title was very unusual in his day, and was not picked up by the early church.)
- Jesus saw his mission as the Son of Man as leading to his death. (The dying of the Son of Man was unprecedented

in Judaism. Even among Jesus' followers it was both un-expected and unwelcome.)

- Jesus, though apparently understanding himself to be Is-rael's promised Messiah, was curiously circumspect about this identification. (This is striking, given the early and widespread confession of Christians that Jesus was the Messiah.)

- Jesus did various sorts of miracles, including healings and "nature miracles."

- At least one of Jesus' miracles involved the multiplica-tion of food so that thousands could eat when they were hungry.

- Jesus even raised the dead.

- The miracles of Jesus were understood as signs of God's power that pointed to truth beyond the miracle itself.

- Jesus was misunderstood by almost everybody, including his own disciples.

- Jewish opponents of Jesus accused him of being empow-ered by supernatural evil.

- Jesus experienced conflict with many Jewish leaders, es-pecially the Pharisees and ultimately the temple-centered leadership in Jerusalem.

- Jesus spoke and acted in ways that undermined the temple in Jerusalem.

- Jesus spoke and acted in ways that implied he had a unique connection with God.

- Jesus referred to God as Father, thus claiming unusual intimacy with God.

- Jesus was crucified in Jerusalem, at the time of Passover, under the authority of Pontius Pilate, and with the coop-eration of some Jewish leaders in Jerusalem. (There are quite a few more details concerning the death of Jesus that are shared by all four Gospels.)

- Most of Jesus' followers either abandoned him or denied him during his crucifixion.

- Jesus was raised from the dead on the first day of the week.

- Women were the first witnesses to the evidence of Jesus' resurrection. (This is especially significant, since the testimony of women was not highly regarded in first-century Jewish culture. Nobody would have made up stories with women as witnesses if they wanted those stories to gain ready acceptance.)

This is certainly an impressive list of similarities shared by all four Gospels. It's especially significant because I've included the Gospel of John here, even though it is the most different among the biblical Gospels. It shows that John shares with the Synoptics the same basic narrative. Thus the four biblical testimonies about Jesus are impressively similar at the core. Because Matthew and Luke used Mark, their witnesses aren't independent, but they do corroborate Mark's account. Thus the fact that there are four Gospels contributes significantly to our confidence in their historical accuracy.

But what about the *differences* among the Gospels? How do they impact our evaluation of the trustworthiness of these writings? Are there contradictions in the Gospels? We'll turn to these questions in the next chapter.

Chapter 9

Are There Contradictions in the Gospels?

In the last chapter I showed that the four New Testament Gospels agree considerably in their depictions of Jesus. In fact, the same essential aspects of Jesus' ministry can be found in all of the Gospels. But that is not to say that the Gospels tell exactly the same story in exactly the same way. In fact, each Gospel views Jesus from a distinctive perspective and provides unique insight into his ministry. This means, of course, that there are many variations among the New Testament Gospels.

I just used the word "variations" for the differences among the Gospels. Others would use language that carries a more negative connotation. When I was in graduate school, my professors tended to speak, not of variations among the Gospels so much as discrepancies or disparities. In some circles, you'll hear about the disagreements or contradictions among the Gospels. For example, some time ago *Time* magazine ran a cover story on the birth of Jesus. The article stated:

Matthew and Luke diverge in conspicuous ways on details of the event. In Matthew's Nativity, the angelic Annunciation is made to Joseph while Luke's is to Mary. Matthew's offers wise men and a star and puts the baby Jesus in a house; Luke's prefers shepherds and a manger. Both place the birth in Bethlehem, but *they disagree totally* about how it came to be there.[1]

Time rightly shows the variations in the nativity stories of Matthew and Luke. But it wrongly adds that the two Gospels "disagree totally" about how the birth came to be in Bethlehem. When I last checked, disagreement or contradiction involves specifically denying something. Saying something differently isn't disagreement, unless of course the two statements couldn't both be true. So the fact that Matthew has Magi and Luke has shepherds is a genuine difference but not a contradiction. If Luke placed the birth of Jesus in Bethlehem, while Matthew favored Nazareth, this would be a contradiction. Or it would be a genuine discrepancy if one Gospel had Jesus die by crucifixion and another had him die by stoning (as is recorded in the Jewish Talmud[2]). There are differences among the Gospel accounts, to be sure. But actual contradictions? I don't think so.

Examples of Differences among the Gospels

Most of the differences among the Gospels are inconsequential matters of word choice or literary emphasis. But there are some differences that cannot be dismissed as trivial. For example, in Matthew Jesus faces three temptations from the devil: 1) "turn stones into bread"; 2) "throw yourself off the temple"; and 3) "worship me" (see Matt. 4:1–11). Luke's narrative also includes three temptations, but in a different order: 1) "stones to bread"; 2) "worship me"; and 3) "throw yourself off the temple" (see Luke 4:1–13). Of course many skeptical scholars would deny the historicity of this whole scene because

---

1. David Van Biema, "Behind the First Noel," *Time*, December 13, 2004, emphasis added, see http://www.time.com/time/archive/preview/0,10987,1009720,00.html.
2. *Talmud, b. Sanh.* 43a.

it involves supernatural elements. But those who accept the possibility that this really happened face the peculiar variation in the order of temptations 2 and 3.

Is this a contradiction? I suppose it is if both Matthew and Luke were intending to present the three temptations in the exact order in which they actually occurred. In this case, either Matthew or Luke would be wrong, and it would be fair to refer to the variation between them as a genuine disagreement. But if Matthew and Luke were seeking to present what really happened but in more of a thematic way rather than in chronological order, then it would be unfair to say they contradict each other.

The Gospel writers did, at times, order events by theme rather than chronology. Consider another example. In Mark 6, well into Jesus' Galilean ministry in this Gospel, there are two crucial events: Jesus' rejection in his hometown of Nazareth (6:1–6) and the arrest and murder of John the Baptist (6:17–29). Yet in the Gospel of Luke, the arrest of John is described in chapter 3, before Jesus begins his ministry (3:20), and the rejection of Jesus in Nazareth is placed at the very beginning of his ministry (4:16–30). If Luke was using Mark, as is likely, then he purposely moved these events for some reason or another. I think the move has to do primarily with dramatic reasons, though it may also reflect theological emphasis. Luke, it seems, didn't believe it was a problem to diverge from Mark's apparent chronology. Nor did the Christians who accepted both Mark and Luke as authoritative.

Seeing such chronological differences between the Gospels, a naysayer might be quick to say, "Aha! So there are contradictions. The Gospels aren't reliable." But as I explained in chapter 7, this would be another case of anachronistic judgment. It's taking our contemporary value of chronology and forcing it upon writers who did not necessarily share it. In fact, historians and biographers in the Hellenistic world often preferred thematic to chronological orderings of events. So the New Testament evangelists were simply doing what came naturally, and what would have been expected by their readers.

We do this sort of thing quite commonly today, though not in the writing of history or biography. Suppose, for example, I was going to tell you what I did on last summer's vacation alongside Swan Lake, Montana. I would be sure to relate much of what I did. But, without checking my journal, I can't remember exactly when I went tubing on the lake, or jumped off the cliff, or went kayaking with my daughter (when we saw a moose only a few yards away!). Chances are I would organize my narrative of the vacation along thematic lines: lake activities, side trips, places we ate, animals we saw, etc. Listening to this account, you wouldn't accuse me of lying about my vacation because you wouldn't expect me to provide a precise, day-by-day version of events.

Asking the Gospels to Be Something They Are Not

Similarly, the first readers of the Gospels wouldn't have expected Matthew, Mark, Luke, and John to narrate all of the events in the precise order in which they happened. That's just not how it was done in those days. So if we come along and insist that, in order to be reliable, the Gospels must get everything in precise chronological order, we're demanding something that is both anachronistic and inconsistent with the intentions of the evangelists. We're asking the Gospels to be something that they are not.

Ironically, this sort of demand has been placed on the Gospels by unlikely bedfellows. Some very conservative Christians have argued that the Gospel accounts must be 100 percent accurate in every last detail, including chronology, in order to be truly God's Word. Thus they fight for the absolute accuracy of every jot and tittle of chronology in the Gospels, believing that one tiny inconsistency brings down the whole authority of the Bible. Ironically, in order to solve the problem of obvious chronological variation, they end up resorting to interpretations that turn the obvious meaning of the Gospels on its head.

On the flip side, many liberal scholars and others who want to undermine biblical authority also agree that the smallest inconsistency—read "contradiction"—in the Gospels invalidates their reliability. In graduate school I was amazed at how quickly some of my professors and fellow students would identify a "contradiction" even before considering ways in which a difference between two Gospel accounts could be responsibly seen as a noncontradictory variation. Thus, both the fundamentalist and the opponent of biblical authority end up making the same kind of mistake when it comes to evaluating the reliability of the Gospels. They apply anachronistic and unfair standards to the Gospels, demanding they be what they were never intended to be. (Note: what I've just said is not true of most leading evangelical scholars today. Many who affirm the authority, even inerrancy of Scripture also take seriously the intentions of the Gospel writers and the literary conventions of their day.)

Common Variations among the Gospels

There are other kinds of relatively common variations among the biblical Gospels. These are neatly and comprehensively catalogued by Craig Blomberg in his fine book *The Historical Reliability of the Gospels*.[3] In a chapter called "Contradictions among the Synoptics?"[4] Blomberg discusses seven main types of supposed contradictions among the Gospels. Here's a summary of his types:

1. Conflicting theology? This category has to do with genuine differences between the theological perspectives of the evangelists, which are understood by some scholars to be in conflict with each other rather than being complementary. Blomberg argues for complementarity.

3. Craig L. Blomberg, *The Historical Reliability of the Gospels* (Downers Grove, Ill.: InterVarsity Press, 1987).
4. Ibid., 113–152.

2. The practice of paraphrase. A verse in one Gospel will be found in similar but not quite the same language in another Gospel.

3. Chronological problems.

4. Omissions. Often one Gospel doesn't include material found in another Gospel. For example, Mark 11:12–24 tells the story of Jesus' cursing of the fig tree. This story is found in Matthew 21 but is not in Luke.

5. Composite speeches. For example, some scholars believe that the Sermon on the Mount, in its present form, was created by Matthew out of individual sayings of Jesus, and not actually spoken by Jesus in the form in which it appears in Matthew.

6. Apparent doublets. These are stories in the Gospels that could be two different versions of the same event, as in the case of the feeding of the 5,000 and the 4,000 (Mark 6:32–44; 8:1–10 and parallels). Of course *apparent* doublets could reflect two different but similar historical events.

7. Variations in names and numbers. Examples would include the name(s) of the place where Jesus cast Legion out of a demonized man (Gerasa? Gadara? Matthew 8:28; Mark 5:1), or the healing of one blind man in Mark 10:46, where Matthew 20:30 seems to tell the same story with two blind men.

Blomberg addresses each of these categories of apparent contradiction, showing in detail why the genuine differences are not truly contradictory.

What Happened to the Roof?

Let me give an example of a difference between the Gospels that might be wrongly styled a contradiction.[5] It illustrates two

5. Blomberg mentions this example (123), though without as much detail as I'm supplying here.

of Blomberg's categories. It's from the story of the healing of the paralytic, where Jesus forgives the man's sins and so gets into trouble with some Jewish leaders (Matt. 9:2–8; Mark 2:1–12; Luke 5:17–26). The essential elements of this story are found in all three Gospels—the healing of the paralyzed man, the forgiveness of sins, the controversy with the leaders—as are many details. But one particular element of Mark's story is different in Matthew and Luke.

Mark's account begins with some people bringing a paralyzed man to Jesus so that he might heal him. But because of the crowds, they couldn't easily get to Jesus. So, according to Mark:

> And when they could not bring him to Jesus because of the crowd, they removed the roof above him; and after having dug through it, they let down the mat on which the paralytic lay (Mark 2:4).

How does this curious detail play out in Matthew and Luke? Matthew omits the digging through the roof part altogether. Why does Matthew do this? We don't really know. Perhaps he was economizing on words. Perhaps he considered this detail unimportant. Perhaps he realized that it might be misunderstood by some readers. For whatever reason, Matthew left out the digging through the roof (and other details as well). Is this difference a contradiction? Hardly.

In Luke's Gospel, however, the roof shows up, though in a curiously different phrasing:

> [B]ut finding no way to bring him in because of the crowd, they went up on the roof and let him down with his bed through the tiles into the middle of the crowd in front of Jesus (Luke 5:19).

In Mark, the paralytic's friends "dug down" through the roof. In Luke they let their friend down "through the tiles." What explains this odd variation? Perhaps Mark's version of the story reflects the fact that typical homes in Galilee in the

107

time of Jesus had thatched roofs through which one could dig. It's likely that Mark's version is more literally accurate. Luke, who is writing for a Gentile audience, changes the imagery to that which would be intelligible to his readers, who would have been familiar with tiled rather than thatched roofs. It seems clear that Luke paraphrased Mark's text so that his readers wouldn't worry about how one "digs through" a tiled roof.

Now, surely, Luke could have let "digs through" remain, and added a note of explanation for his readers. This is the kind of thing I would do today if I were describing the healing of the paralytic. But I have different standards for history writing than Luke had. If I were to say that Luke made a mistake, or that he contradicted Mark, then I'd be showing myself as a poor historian, since I would fail to take seriously the cultural values of Luke's day.

Though it's common in many scholarly circles to speak of "contradictions" as "the assured results of scholarship," in fact many if not all of the so-called "contradictions" in the Bible have been carefully analyzed and interpreted by scholars who have then concluded that true contradictions don't exist. Many of the apparent contradictions turn out to depend on superficial or rigid readings of the text. Yet efforts to harmonize the Gospel accounts are sometimes rejected as quaint remnants of an earlier day rather than as legitimate efforts by historians to determine the true meaning of the Gospel texts. To be sure, some proposed harmonizations are unpersuasive if not downright silly, but many deserve to be taken more seriously.

At the same time, some people—both conservative and liberal—have been reticent to take seriously the nature of the Gospels as understood within their own time and culture. If it's true that the Gospel writers were doing what biographers and historians were expected to do in the first-century Greco-Roman world, then we shouldn't be surprised to find plenty of variations between the Gospels. So, to return to the example I noted previously, where Luke appears to change Mark's thatched roof to a tiled roof, some conservative scholars would no doubt try to solve this apparent inconsistency by claiming that the roof had both thatched and tiled portions, or that one could be said to "dig" through tiles, or something to ensure that both Mark and Luke are literally accurate. But these efforts are misguided, in my opinion. They force Luke into a modern mold that defines historical accuracy in a way different from Luke's own definition.

This does an injustice to Luke, and ultimately, in my view, to the Bible itself. It says, "I insist that the Gospels must be what I want them to be (or what my culture wants them to be, or what my theology wants them to be)," rather than "I receive the Gospels as they are, and will not require them to be something they are not." If God chose to work through biographers who, like their Hellenistic peers, paraphrased sayings or ordered events thematically rather than chronologically, who am I to say this is wrong? Isn't that asking not only Luke but even the Lord to conform to the values of my own culture, rather than accepting God's choice to work within the constraints of another culture? Indeed, there's a part of me that wishes God had waited to send his Son until he could have been captured on videotape! But I trust that the Lord chose just the right time to come in the flesh, even if this means I don't get the sort of accuracy and detail in the presentation of the life of Christ that I might prefer.

The Distinctiveness of the Gospel of John

When we take seriously the nature of history and biography writing in the first century A.D., and when we treat Matthew, Mark, and Luke as first-century biographies, and when we deal with their differences seriously rather than glibly, it makes little sense to speak of "contradictions" between the Gospels. For all of their distinctiveness, the Synoptic Gospels tell more or less the same story of Jesus in more or less the same way.

But the Gospel of John? Aye, there's the rub! The fourth Gospel stands apart from the Synoptics in many ways. True, the essential story of Jesus is found in this Gospel as in the others.

And, true, the differences between John and the Synoptics have often been overstated. But, after browsing through Matthew, Mark, and Luke, where, for the most part, Jesus utters short parables and pithy sayings, even the casual reader is struck by how different Jesus sounds in John. The short sayings have been replaced by much longer discourses. The primary message of the kingdom of God, though present in John, doesn't take the spotlight. Instead, in the fourth Gospel Jesus speaks much more of himself and his relationship with his Father. Here Jesus is the bread of life and the light of the world. He is the good shepherd and the vine to which his disciples must stay connected. Plus, in John, the apparent chronology and travelogue of Jesus' ministry are more complicated, with several trips between Galilee and Jerusalem. (Ironically, even many hyper-critical scholars regard John's timetable as fairly accurate.)

For some, the obvious differences between John and the Synoptics clearly diminish the historical reliability of John. (A few have argued that John is older and more authentic, but they are a small minority.) If Matthew, Mark, and Luke more or less get Jesus right, the argument goes, then John clearly gets him wrong, from a historical point of view. The speeches of Jesus in the fourth Gospel, it is claimed, reflect a long tradition of development within the community that ultimately produced this Gospel. They have little to do with the real Jesus.

When I was in graduate school, this perspective reigned in the academic circles in which I danced. But even then there was a growing recognition that John, while distinctive, might actually preserve genuine, independent traditions about Jesus. Why, it was asked, must we assume that Jesus always spoke only in short quips? Didn't it make sense to believe that, in some settings, he spoke in longer discourses? And wasn't it possible that John, though reflecting decades of tradition, actually preserved some of these discourses? Moreover, given that most critical scholars believed that John used older written sources, the later date proposed for the fourth Gospel (80s or 90s A.D.) didn't mean that its content was historically unreliable.

110

Not surprisingly, several conservative scholars have risen to defend the historical reliability of John. None has been more prolific in this regard than Craig Blomberg. His book *The Historical Reliability of John's Gospel: Issues and Commentary* devotes 346 dense pages to defending the historicity of John's portrayal of Jesus. Blomberg is not a naïve harmonizer. He takes seriously the distinctiveness of John's Gospel. This distinctiveness accounts for the differences between John and the Synoptics but it doesn't require denigrating the historical reliability of either. Blomberg's conclusion, after a long investigation, is that "one may affirm with considerable confidence that John's Gospel is true—not merely theologically . . . but also historically."[6]

Jesus and Half Dome: Four Revealing Pictures

Of course for this approach to succeed, one needs to grant that the pictures of Jesus in the New Testament Gospels aren't precise photographs so much as inspired paintings. If you've spent much time looking at paintings, you know that many are not "literal" in the photographic sense. Yet a great painting can capture a slice of reality that eludes the photographer. It can convey mood, feeling, and insight. And it can be profoundly "true" without being literalistic.

Consider, for example, the four "paintings" following page 96. You probably recognize these as different representations of Half Dome, the mammoth granite monolith that dwarfs the eastern end of Yosemite Valley in California. A couple of the paintings are more literal; a couple more suggestive. None looks exactly like a photograph. Yet it would be wrong to criticize the paintings because they aren't photographic enough.

If you saw only one of these paintings of Half Dome, you would have an idea what it really looks like. In fact, if you had never seen it before, either in person or in pictures, and you went

6. Craig L. Blomberg, *The Historical Reliability of John's Gospel: Issues and Commentary* (Downers Grove, Ill.: InterVarsity Press, 2001), 294.

to Yosemite Valley, from one painting alone you would be able to identify Half Dome. Yet if you had seen all four paintings, you would have an even better idea of what Half Dome really looks like in all of its subtlety and variety.

So it is with Jesus and the Gospels. If you had access to only one of the four Gospels, you would have a trustworthy picture of Jesus. It wouldn't be as detailed or as literal as a photograph. But you could trust it to reveal the truth about Jesus. With four Gospels, you're able to see different things in Jesus and to know with greater accuracy what he was really like.

Differences among the Gospels . . . Old News!

Sometimes scholars talk as if recognition of the differences among the Gospels is a recent discovery. They can think they've discovered some new secret that has the power to undermine Christian confidence in Scripture. But in fact this is not a secret at all. Differences among the Gospels have been recognized for as long as Christians have been reading these documents synoptically, well back into the second century A.D.

Sometime around A.D. 180 Irenaeus wrote his treatise *Against Heresies*. Here Irenaeus not only referred to the four New Testament Gospels as authoritative but also attested to the differences among them. In a rather lengthy passage, he used the four living creatures in Revelation 4:5–11—lion, ox, human, eagle—as symbols for the Gospels, noting how the symbols capture unique qualities of each Gospel:

> It is not possible that the Gospels can be either more or fewer in number than they are. . . . For the cherubim, too, were four-faced, and their faces were images of the dispensation of the Son of God. For, [as the Scripture] says, "The first living creature was like a lion," symbolizing His effectual working, His leadership, and royal power; the second [living creature] was like a calf, signifying [His] sacrificial and sacerdotal order; but "the third had, as it were, the face as of a man,"—an evident description of His advent as a human being; "the fourth was like a flying

112

eagle," pointing out the gift of the Spirit hovering with His wings over the Church. And therefore the Gospels are in accord with these things, among which Christ Jesus is seated. For that according to John relates His original, effectual, and glorious generation from the Father, thus declaring, "In the beginning was the Word, and the Word was with God, and the Word was God." Also, "all things were made by Him, and without Him was nothing made." For this reason, too, is that Gospel full of all confidence, for such is His person. But that according to Luke, taking up [His] priestly character, commenced with Zacharias the priest offering sacrifice to God. For now was made ready the fatted calf, about to be immolated for the finding again of the younger son. Matthew, again, relates His generation as a man, saying, "The book of the generation of Jesus Christ, the son of David, the son of Abraham;" and also, "The birth of Jesus Christ was on this wise." This, then, is the Gospel of His humanity; for which reason it is, too, that [the character of] a humble and meek man is kept up through the whole Gospel. Mark, on the other hand, commences with [a reference to] the prophetical spirit coming down from on high to men, saying, "The beginning of the Gospel of Jesus Christ, as it is written in Esaias the prophet,"—pointing to the winged aspect of the Gospel; and on this account he made a compendious and cursory narrative, for such is the prophetical character.[7]

Irenaeus exemplifies the fact that Christians have recognized from the earliest times that the four biblical Gospels are distinctive. Rather than disguising this fact with a single harmony, as attempted by Tatian with his *Diatessaron*, they celebrated the differences as part of God's revelation.

Letting the Gospels Be Messy

It is also worth noting that the second-century Christians didn't "clean up" the four Gospels. It's true that some of the scribes did harmonize divergent texts, so there would be fewer differences among the Gospels. But, by and large, the church

7. Irenaeus, *Against Heresies* 3.11.8.

kept the original texts intact, even though this meant preserving some of the very elements that could be labeled as "contradictions." This fact suggests two implications.

First, it confirms the judgment that people in the Hellenistic world didn't expect historical or biographical works to get every word exactly right. Second-century believers could accept Matthew, Mark, Luke, and John as authoritative accounts of Jesus' life, even though there were acknowledged variations among them.

Second, the fact that the church did not prefer a single harmonized Gospel, but instead kept the four distinct ones, suggests that the early Christians did indeed seek to preserve accurately the written accounts of Jesus' life, even though they were aware of the differences among these accounts. To put it differently, there was no conspiracy in the early church to clean up the Gospels. The truth needed to be protected and preserved, even if it was messy.

I'm aware that what I've just said flows upstream in some rivers of biblical scholarship. It is common to hear scholars argue that the Gospels are primarily theological documents, and therefore were not meant to be historically accurate in the first place. Theology and history, it seems, are incompatible. In the next chapter I'll take up this issue. If it turns out that the motivations of the evangelists were more theological than academic, if they were promoting a religious agenda more than writing history for antiquarian reasons, does this discount the reliability of the Gospels?

Chapter 10

If the Gospels Are Theology, Can They Be History?

If there's one thing all New Testament scholars agree on, it's the fact that the Gospels were not written merely for reasons of historical curiosity. The most liberal critic and the most conservative commentator, and everyone in between, would surely agree that Matthew, Mark, Luke, and John were not writing simply out of antiquarian interest. They weren't scholars who found Jesus fascinating and decided to write about his life to further their careers. Rather, they were faithful believers in Jesus who composed narratives of his ministry for theological reasons. In the language of our contentious world, the Gospel writers had an agenda. They were writing theology, not raw history (as if there were such a thing).

No Hidden Agenda

None of the evangelists had a *hidden* agenda, however. Each writer revealed quite plainly his theological inclination as well as his personal faith in Jesus. Matthew begins his narrative by referring to Jesus as "the Messiah, the son of David, the son of Abraham" (1:1). Not exactly the vocabulary of a neutral observer! Similarly, Mark starts his Gospel in this way: "The beginning of the good news of Jesus Christ, the Son of God" (1:1). Mark is telling a story he believes to be "good news," and it concerns Jesus, whom Mark believes to be the "Christ" and "the Son of God." (By the way, Mark speaks of the beginning of the "good news," which in Greek is *euangelion*, or "Gospel." This is probably the origin of the use of "Gospel" as the genre for the four biblical biographies of Jesus. Mark himself probably didn't use "Gospel" in this way, however, but rather as a summary of the content of his biographical narrative. English translations that use "Gospel" in Mark 1:1 run the risk of missing Mark's meaning.)

Luke is even clearer about the purpose of his narrative. In an introduction reminiscent of the secular historians who may have inspired Luke, he begins:

> Since many have undertaken to set down an orderly account of the events that have been fulfilled among us, just as they were handed on to us by those who from the beginning were eyewitnesses and servants of the word, I too decided, after investigating everything carefully from the very first, to write an orderly account for you, most excellent Theophilus, so that you may know the truth concerning the things about which you have been instructed (Luke 1:1–4).

Luke is writing an orderly account of the events concerning Jesus so that Luke's reader might "know the truth" about faith in Christ. More literally, Luke is claiming to help his reader have "certainty" about the one in whom he believes. This is not academic history so much as intentional discipleship. It is teaching meant to help a believer grow in his faith.

116

The purpose of the fourth Gospel is also plainly stated, though near the end of the book rather than at its beginning:

> Now Jesus did many other signs in the presence of his disciples, which are not written in this book. But these are written so that you may come to believe that Jesus is the Messiah, the Son of God, and that through believing you may have life in his name (John 20:30–31).

According to this translation (NRSV), John's primary purpose is evangelistic. He wrote "so that you *may come to believe* that Jesus is the Messiah, the Son of God." The Gospel of John may in fact be the first evangelistic tract in human history.[1] The fourth Gospel, like the Synoptics, has an openly stated theological agenda.

What I've said about the intentions of the Gospel writers is confirmed by the Gospels themselves. In the way they are structured, in the emphases of the stories, in the presentation of miracles, and in the stunning conclusion on Easter and thereafter, Matthew, Mark, Luke, and John show their theological purposes. The Gospels are, without a doubt, theologically motivated writings, composed for pastoral, evangelistic, or apologetic purposes, or some combination of the three.

The "Ugly, Broad Ditch"

So, if the evangelists were faithful believers in Jesus seeking to perpetuate or promote the faith, if they had admitted

---

1. Ironically, John 20:31 is one of those rare verses in the New Testament where the actual Greek text isn't completely clear in one key place. If you were to look at the Greek behind the phrase "you may come to believe," you would see something like this: *pisteu[s]ete*. The brackets were not in the original text, of course. They were added by the editors of the Greek text to indicate uncertainty about whether the original word was *pisteuete* or *pisteusete*. The first is in the present tense, the second in a past tense (aorist). Why does this matter? If John originally used *pisteusete*, then the translation "that you may come to believe" is correct, and the Gospel is meant to lead nonbelievers to faith. But if he used *pisteuete*, then the translation should be "that you may continue believing," in which case the Gospel is meant to encourage Christians to keep on in the faith. Either way, John's intent is either pastoral or evangelistic, or perhaps both.

theological agendas, can we still regard them as historically reliable? At this point in the conversation many scholars say no. Theology precludes history, or so we're told.

When I took my first New Testament course in college, I was shocked by the extent to which my professor denied the historical reliability of the Gospels. Yet I knew Professor Mac-Rae was an ordained priest who sometimes did pastoral things, like preach or administer the sacraments. So when I found out that he was preaching in Harvard's chapel, I was eager to attend. That's when I got the next shock from this professor. His sermon, though hardly evangelistic, articulated orthodox truth from the perspective of Christian faith.

Leaving that worship service, I felt terribly confused. How could one who believed so little in the classroom believe so much in the chapel? How could he affirm so confidently that for which he saw so little historical basis? It was almost as if his faith were completely disconnected from history, and impervious to the skepticism of the academy, even his own skepticism.

What I did not realize at the time was that my professor stood in a long line of similarly minded theologians stretching back to the eighteenth century. Gotthold Ephraim Lessing (1729–1781), a German best known for his plays, sought to defend Christian faith against skeptical historians who were chipping away at it. Lessing argued that theology can never be dependent upon history, because theology has to do with eternal truths which can be known only by reason, while history produces only contingent knowledge. In his most famous phrase, Lessing argued that there is an "ugly, broad ditch" that separates history and theology (German, *der garstige breite Graben*).

Lessing profoundly influenced theology in the years to come, providing the intellectual foundation for my first New Testament professor's ability to separate history and theology. It enabled him to say things like, "As a Christian I can believe in the virginal conception of Jesus, but as a historian I operate on the assumption that there are no children born without natural fathers." Theology on one side, history on the other, and an ugly, broad ditch between them.

Given that much of New Testament scholarship in the last century has been done by scholars under the influence of Lessing, we shouldn't be surprised that theologians tend to answer negatively the question I've been asking in this chapter: If the Gospels are theology, can they be history? Theology and history are different things altogether, it is assumed. So if Matthew, Mark, Luke, and John were writing theology, if they had religious agendas, then we shouldn't expect their work to be historically reliable. For these writers, it is argued, theology trumps history.

Theology Based on History

Of course it's certainly possible for theology to be based on something other than events that can be studied by historians. The myths that underlie ancient Greek religion, for example, didn't really happen. Moreover, even in Scripture there are fictional stories that convey profound theological truths. There needn't have been a real-life Good Samaritan for Jesus' theological point about love to be both true and compelling. In this case, and many more like it, theology is independent of history.

Yet the Gospels present themselves as something other than expanded fictional parables. Luke is clearest in this regard, by beginning his Gospel with a prologue that intentionally echoes the prologues of other historians from his era. Moreover, for centuries almost all orthodox Christians have taken the biblical Gospels as reliable narratives of what Jesus actually did and said, even though many of these Christians have seen far more than mere history in the Gospel narratives. (For example, an allegorical approach to the Gospels was popular for many centuries.)

The evangelists wrote reliable history because they cared about what had happened in the past. And why did they care

119

about the past? Because their theology was anchored in past events. After all, one cannot very well believe that salvation came through the atoning death of Jesus if that death didn't really happen. A nice story about a dying Messiah just wouldn't cut it. In the prologue to his Gospel, John wrote, "And the Word became flesh and lived among us, and we have seen his glory, the glory as of a father's only son, full of grace and truth" (1:14). Undeniably, this is a theological affirmation. But it is theology melded with history (he "lived among us"). Moreover, it's theology that leads one to care about history. Believe that Jesus was really God in the flesh and you'll pay close attention to what he actually did and said.

If the evangelists had had a theology like that of G. E. Lessing, if they had viewed history and theology as distinct, then they wouldn't have cared a whit about history. In fact, they never would have bothered to write their Gospels. But Matthew, Mark, Luke, and John didn't have the benefit of Lessing's "wisdom." They, like the vast majority of Jews before them and Christians after them, believed that what actually happened made all the difference in the world. It was in the realm of history that God made his presence known, revealing himself and his salvation. Therefore history wasn't inessential. It was at the heart of the evangelists' theology.

In this regard the Gospel writers were quite similar to the apostle Paul. In his first letter to the Christians in Corinth, Paul dealt with the view that resurrections, including the resurrection of Jesus, don't happen. Here's what he wrote:

> If there is no resurrection of the dead, then Christ has not been raised; and if Christ has not been raised, then our proclamation has been in vain and your faith has been in vain (1 Cor. 15:13–14).

In other words, it isn't nearly enough to regard the story of Jesus' resurrection as an inspiring fiction, or a symbolic rendering of some ahistorical reality. Paul said, "If Christ has not been raised," in space-time reality, then Christian faith isn't true.

What happened to Jesus has everything to do with theology. As it is with Paul, so also with the Gospel writers.

Truthful History Motivated by Theology

Sometimes I find it odd that certain scholars have so much trouble seeing how history and theology are intertwined, and how one with a theological agenda can, in fact, labor faithfully to pass on reliable history. This is hard for me to fathom because, frankly, I am motivated all the time by a theological passion that calls me to be a faithful historian.

Virtually every weekend I preach a sermon in the four worship services at Irvine Presbyterian Church. I freely admit that my sermons reflect my theological agenda. I want my congregants to grow in their faith. And, at the same time, I'm seeking to encourage non-Christians to put their faith in Christ. So I have a clear, open, and passionate theological agenda. No question about it. Agenda-less preaching would be drivel.

My agenda leads me to tell stories because I believe stories communicate powerfully in today's world. Most of my stories concern events that really happened, either in my own life or in the lives of people I know, though sometimes I use items that have appeared in the news or other sources. When I tell a true story, I make every effort to get the crucial facts right. This also reflects my "agenda," because I believe that my congregation will trust me if I am a reliable historian. Moreover, my theology tells me that truth matters.

My commitment to telling the truth means that when I hear some wonderful story from a friend or from the Internet, I work hard to verify its truthfulness before I use it in a sermon. Sometimes the most heartrending stories turn out to be fictitious. A notable example is the tale of little Teddy Stallard (or Stoddard), the disadvantaged student who became a success because of the love of a teacher, Miss Thompson. This saga has been used in hundreds of sermons, sometimes by pastors who talk as if they know Teddy personally. But, alas, Teddy is a fictional character, made up in a short story by Elizabeth Ballard.[2]

My Agenda-Driven Story

My theological agenda also motivates me to be truthful when I'm telling a story from my own life. Here's an example of a story I've used in a sermon:

When I was a sophomore in college, I wanted to share my Christian faith with others. But, as an introverted person, I wasn't likely to walk up to a stranger or even a friend and get into a conversation about God. So I decided to pray and ask the Lord to help me.

One brisk Saturday evening in October, I decided to go down to Harvard Square and see if I could share my faith with somebody. The Square was filled with students from all over the Boston area, and it seemed a likely place for God to drop a seeker into my lap. I prayed earnestly for God to guide me to someone with whom I could talk openly about Christianity. "Lord," I prayed, "you know I'm pretty shy about this. So it would be great if you would work a little miracle here, and find me somebody with whom I could share. And if you could make it obvious, that would be really helpful." With this prayer in my heart, I set off for the Square.

I wandered around for a while, wondering where "my person" was. "Lord," I kept on praying, "please bring me somebody who wants to learn about you." Still nothing happened. After a half hour or so I began to feel both discouraged and silly.

Just then, two young women approached me. "We're going to a party at Dunster House," they explained, "but we don't know how to get there. Could you help us?"

"Sure," I said. "Glad to." Meanwhile I thought to myself, "This is great. Not only has God brought these people into

2. For more on little Teddy, see my web site: http://www.markdroberts/htmfiles/archives/9.1.04–9.30.04.htm#sep2404.

my life so I can talk to them about my faith, but they happen to be two attractive women. God, you've outdone yourself this time!" Dunster House was about a ten-minute walk from Harvard Square, so I figured this would be plenty of time to engage these women in a conversation about God.

On the walk down to Dunster, I kept bringing up subjects that I felt sure would lead to a conversation about God. "I'm majoring in philosophy," I said, "Are you interested in philosophy?"

They weren't.

"Sometimes I wonder why we're here on this earth. Do you ever think about this?"

They didn't.

Basically, they wanted to party at Dunster House, not reflect on the meaning of life with their overly earnest tour guide. For ten minutes I tried everything I could think of to get the women to talk about God. Nothing doing. Of the thousands of students in Cambridge that night, they were the least interested in God.

When we got to Dunster House, I walked them to the door. They thanked me and left. I felt like a complete idiot. "Okay, God," I prayed, "I get the point. You've probably had a good chuckle over my silliness. Well, that's enough. I'm going home. This was a stupid idea." I left the entrance to Dunster House and headed back to my dorm.

Just then I passed a student I recognized as being a friend of a friend. He said "Hi" so I returned the greeting as we went off in opposite directions. All of a sudden he stopped, turned around, and called to me, "Hey, are you Mark Roberts?"

"Yes," I said, surprised that he knew my name.

"Well, I'm Matt. I'm a friend of your roommate Bob."

"Oh, yeah. Hello, Matt," I said.

"I've been wanting to talk to you," Matt said.

"Me?" I asked incredulously. "Why me?"

"Because I hear you're a Christian. *I need to talk to you about God.*"

And so began a conversation that lasted well into the night. That conversation turned into a weekly Bible study, as Matt and I looked into the Gospels to find out about Jesus. When we finished, Matt wasn't ready to give his life to Christ. But he was closer than he had been on that strange night when we met on the walk outside of Dunster House. End of story.

To the best of my forty-nine-year-old memory, I have faithfully related the essence of this story: my desire to share my faith and my prayer for divine help; my meeting with the two women; our Dunster House destination; my "chance" meeting with Mike and his words to me. When I used this story in a sermon, my theological "agenda" motivated me to get the basic facts right. But it also helped me shape the telling of the story, choosing which facts were important and which were not. I did not, for example, say anything about how the women I escorted were dressed (in preppy sweaters) or where they went to school (Wellesley College), because these tidbits didn't contribute to the point of the story.

Now, I must confess, I did include a few "facts" that I'm not completely sure of. I said this happened on a "brisk Saturday evening in October." In truth, I don't remember if it was a Friday or a Saturday, and I'm not sure if it was in October or November. It was quite cool, this I remember, and I'm positive it was in the fall.

I also supplied a fair amount of dialogue in this story. Honestly, I don't remember the exact words (*ipsissima verba*) with which I prayed, or the exact questions I asked the women as I escorted them to Dunster House. I've truly captured the basic sense of those conversations (*ipsissima vox*), but most of the words have long since escaped my memory. On the contrary, what Matt said to me is burned into my memory. I can still hear him say, "I need to talk to you about God." This was, as you can imagine, one of the most surprising and wonderful things I had ever heard. It was like a dream come true, as God answered my prayer so specifically and obviously.

I should add that "Matt" is not the name of the student I ran into outside of Dunster. I remember his real name, but when I tell stories like this, I often change names to protect the confidentiality of those involved. In this particular case I could safely have used "Matt's" real name, of course, but usually I need to be careful. My congregation understands that I change names sometimes.

In conclusion, did my theological agenda lead me to tell this story in a sermon? Yes. Did my agenda help me choose what to include and what to exclude from this story? Yes. Did my agenda preclude me from being a good historian? Decidedly not. I'm quite certain that this event happened in more or less the way I've narrated it (with the exceptions I've mentioned above). In fact, my agenda as a preacher motivated me to tell this story, to tell it in a certain way, and *to make sure that the essential elements were absolutely truthful*. My theology led me to be a trustworthy historian.

If you were to discover that, in fact, my story of the miraculous encounter with Matt was just a nice little piece of religious fiction, then the power of the story would vanish. After all, what makes it so compelling is the fact that, after I had prayed to share my faith with someone, a virtual stranger said to me, "I need to talk with you about God." This is either a fabrication, an incredible coincidence, or a miracle of God. I vote for miracle.

Speaking of a miracle, we have now come to one of the major problems relating to the reliability of the Gospels. How can we believe that narratives so full of miracles are historically accurate? To this question we'll turn in the next chapter.

Chapter 11

Do Miracles Undermine the Reliability of the Gospels?

I'm a natural-born skeptic. I admit it. For example, if I hear some Christian claim that a miracle has happened, my first impulse isn't to rejoice but to doubt. It isn't that I don't believe miracles occur. In fact I do. But I'm all too aware of how people can exaggerate, or be carried away by emotion, or even fall prey to deception. People today are so eager for some sign of supernatural power, whether divine, angelic, or paranormal, that they'll often see miracles where folks like me would see coincidence, malfeasance, or merely good luck.

My skepticism about the miraculous was nourished by my senior thesis in college. A philosophy major, I chose to write on the famous—some would say infamous—argument against miracles put forth by the eighteen-century philosopher David Hume. My thesis, "The Miraculous Philosophy of David Hume,"[1] was not a refutation of Hume's argument. Rather, I attempted to dissect this classic case against miracles by carefully exegeting section 10 of Hume's *Enquiry Concerning Human Understanding*, viewing this argument in light of the cultural and philosophical milieu in which Hume wrote. His basic point was that the case for miracles is intrinsically weak, given the very nature of the miraculous. If you tell me, for example, that you became invisible at work today, I will not believe you because I have no experience of people becoming invisible, but I do have experience of people deceiving themselves or trying to deceive me. Thus, as a good Humean, I would find deception more likely than invisibility.

Yet, in spite of my innate and well-nourished skepticism, I do not believe that the presence of miracle stories in the Gospels makes them unreliable, though it does complicate the evaluation of their historicity. If there were no miracles in the New Testament Gospels, then many scholars today as well as many ordinary folk would be much more likely to acknowledge the Gospels' historical reliability. Of course, if there were no miracles in the New Testament Gospels, there would be no New Testament Gospels. In fact, there would be no New Testament at all. Jesus would have been dismissed by his contemporaries as an overly optimistic but deceived prophet who proclaimed the kingdom of God but didn't deliver on his promises. His death by crucifixion would have been the end of things. Jesus would quickly have been forgotten as one more wannabe Messiah who failed at the job. Scholarly efforts to take away the miraculous from the Gospels inevitably fail to be persuasive because, like it or not, the narratives of Jesus' ministry are filled with supernatural events. His message and his miracles go hand in hand.

In the rest of this chapter I will suggest seven theses concerning miracles and the Gospels. As you can imagine, I'll just

---

1. Mark David Roberts, "The miraculous philosophy of David Hume: a study of Section X: 'Of miracles,' in Hume's *An Enquiry Concerning Human Understanding.*" Thesis A.B., Honors. Harvard University, 1979.

scratch the surface of this issue. If you're looking for a more in-depth analysis, several books tackle this subject admirably.[2]

1. One's belief about God directly impacts one's evaluation of the miracles in the Gospels.

I am a theist who accepts the theoretical possibility of miracles, and therefore I am open to the possibility that the miracles in the Gospels actually occurred. I believe that there is a Supreme Being, One who created all things, and who can, if he wishes, do things within his creation that are extraordinary. Thus I believe miracles can happen.

If you are not a theist, and you don't believe in the possibility of miracles, then you have no option but to reject the historical reliability of the Gospels. A few scholars have tried to "naturalize" the miracles of Jesus, explaining healings as a matter of psychosomatic suggestion, for example. Most recently, a professor of oceanography seriously argued that Jesus didn't walk on liquid water, but on ice.[3] But this naturalistic approach to the miracles of Jesus hasn't been persuasive, either to most scholars or to most lay people.

2. Miracles do not contradict science.

It is common for people to claim that miracles *cannot* occur because they are contrary to science. But, in fact, miracles aren't contrary to science so much as they are outside of the realm of science. Science studies natural events. Miracles, by definition, are not natural but super-natural. Thus science has nothing to say about them. Now it's true, of course, that many scientists have naturalistic worldviews, in which no supernatural being

2. Craig L. Blomberg, *The Historical Reliability of the Gospels* (Downers Grove, Ill.: InterVarsity Press, 1987), chapter 3; R. Douglas Geivett and Gary R. Habermas, eds., *In Defense of Miracles: A Comprehensive Case for God's Actions in History* (Downers Grove, Ill.: InterVarsity Press, 1997); Graham H. Twelftree, *Jesus the Miracle Worker: A Historical and Theological Study* (Downers Grove, Ill.: InterVarsity Press, 1999).

3. http://www.physorg.com/news63367761.html.

exists. So, naturally, they deny the possibility of miracles. But this is not something they can defend scientifically. It is a philosophical position, not a scientific one. So-called "scientific" rejection of miracles is really more a matter of faith than reason. There are also many theistic scientists who allow that miracles might occur. I have several of these in my own church, including professors and others with Ph.D.'s in natural science.

3. A worldview that includes supernatural powers makes the best sense of some of life's mysteries.

I'm fully aware that, throughout history, people have credited or blamed "the gods" for unexplained natural events. And I'm also willing to concede that there may be many more natural powers than we currently understand or acknowledge. But certain kinds of phenomena are best explained in light of the existence of supernatural beings, both good and evil. I'm thinking here, not only of well-established divine miracles, which are plentiful throughout the world today, but also of demonic realities.[4]

Many things in my life and ministry have been so exceptional, so coincidental, and so wonderful that I cannot account for them apart from belief in a benevolent, miracle-working God. The story in the last chapter about Matt is one example.

4. The "parallels" to the miracles of Jesus found outside of the Bible do not undermine the authenticity of the New Testament accounts, and in many cases they actually support the reliability of the Gospel stories.

It is common for skeptics to argue that the existence of miracle stories in the literature of the Hellenistic world somehow invalidates the historical reliability of the Gospels. People in

---

4. For an expanded discussion of the reality of demons, see my web series *Do Demons Exist?* http://www.markdroberts.com/htmfiles/onetruegodblog/dodemons .htm.

the Greco-Roman world told fantastic stories, not only about gods like Hercules but also about famous humans, like Apollonius of Tyana, a first-century, wonder-working philosopher. It is suggested that the early Christians, aware of these tales, sought to make Jesus competitive in the marketplace of Hellenistic superheroes and therefore invented stories demonstrating his supernatural prowess.

On the surface, this account of the origin of the Gospel miracles seems solid. But a peek beneath the surface shows it to be full of holes. For one thing, most of the stories of miracles in pagan religions were far more fantastic and removed from everyday experience. Unlike Hercules, for example, Jesus didn't slay any multiheaded monsters. The miracles of Jesus dealt with relatively ordinary circumstances, like sickness or hunger.

Moreover, the pagan miracles were often described in an exaggerated, entertaining style. The miracles of Jesus, by contrast, are understated. Furthermore, the Gospels record situations in which Jesus actually lacked supernatural knowledge (Mark 5:30) or power (Mark 6:1–6). In other instances his efforts at exorcism (Mark 5:1–8) and healing (Mark 8:22–26) didn't at first succeed. If the early Christians were making up miracle stories about Jesus, they could have done a much better job, both in content and in form. And surely the Gospel writers, if they were so concerned to polish Jesus' image as the superlative wonder worker, should have tidied up the stories that tarnished that image. But they didn't.

The whole "pagan influence" theory of the Gospel miracles forgets that the first Christians were not Gentiles competing with Hercules and Apollonius of Tyana, but Jews who believed that Jesus was Israel's Messiah. The oral traditions about Jesus' miracles emerged from a predominantly Jewish milieu. If the stories of Jesus' miracles had in fact been fabricated by the first Christians, it's unlikely they would have used pagan models. Old Testament exemplars, like the miracles of Moses or Elijah, would have served the purposes of the first Christians much better.

131

Now there are some fantastic and obviously fictitious miracle stories about Jesus. It's quite likely that these were invented to help Jesus compete successfully with the other philosophers and gods of the Hellenistic world. These Christian stories appear, not in the biblical Gospels, however, but in the noncanonical imitations. In the so-called *Infancy Gospel of Thomas*, for example, Jesus magically lengthens a board that his father cut too short, and raises a playmate from the dead after he died from an accidental fall. The more you read the miracle stories in the post-biblical Gospels, the more you'll be impressed by the reserved and understated character of the New Testament accounts. Of course if you don't believe miracles are possible, then you won't be inclined to accept the New Testament accounts as reliable, but you'll have to admit that they're much less obviously fantastic, in form, style, and substance, than their noncanonical and pagan counterparts.

5. When it comes to reasons for accepting the Gospel miracles as historically accurate, the resurrection leads the way, however ironically.

An argument for the historicity of the Gospel miracles rests on several factors, including, but not limited to: the generally reliable character of the Gospels, the modesty of the miracle stories, the surprising "lapse" in Jesus' powers at some points, and the simple fact that the miracles of Jesus accounted for his widespread popularity. But it wouldn't make sense to argue that any one of Jesus' miracles was solely responsible for the historic rise of Christianity.

Except for the resurrection. Take away the resurrection of Jesus, and you'll have a devil of a time making sense of Christian origins. Jesus died a most shameful death, to all appearances ending his brief stint as a messianic pretender. Nobody in his time, other than Jesus himself, had any place for a suffering, dying Messiah. After Jesus' demise, his disciples were a devastated, frightened bunch who had lost all hope. But then, only a short time thereafter, they became a fearless band of evangelists who ended up changing the course of history. Their message, strangely enough, was that the crucified Jesus had indeed been Israel's Messiah, and that through him God was inaugurating his kingdom. All of this was predicated on a singular conviction: that Jesus had been raised from the dead, and that he was alive, not as a resuscitated corpse, and not as a symbol of spiritual rebirth, but as the living Lord.

What explains the counterintuitive rise of early Christianity? The resurrection, plain and simple. Of course it isn't nearly so simple for scholars who either disbelieve in the possibility of resurrection or who believe that good scholars just can't figure something like the resurrection into their historical explanations, even if they accept such things in their personal faith. But, in my opinion, all efforts to explain why the defeated disciples became enthusiastic evangelists fall short apart from the resurrection. The simplest, most elegant, and most compelling account of the origin of Christianity rests upon this unprecedented miracle.[5]

Why would a natural-born skeptic like me believe that Jesus actually rose from the dead? I believe it because this offers the best account of the birth of Christianity, and the only one I find persuasive. Of course the fact that I'm a theist supports my willingness to accept what otherwise I would deny as impossible. Yet it certainly helps that nonmiraculous and nontheistic theories of Christian origins are so unpersuasive.[6] And once I've allowed that the Gospels faithfully narrate the resurrection

5. For an extraordinarily persuasive (and lengthy) exposition of this point, see N. T. Wright, *The Resurrection of the Son of God* (Minneapolis: Augsburg/Fortress, 2003). For an excellent and much shorter explanation of the importance of the resurrection, see chapter 6, "The Rising of the Son of God and the Birth of the Church," in Ben Witherington III, *New Testament History: A Narrative Account* (Grand Rapids, Mich.: Baker, 2001), 160–187.

6. Such theories include: 1) Early Christians experienced mass hysteria. 2) Somebody stole the body of Jesus, and Christians were fooled. 3) Early Christians had a sense that Jesus lived on in their midst and referred to this as his resurrection. None of these theories accounts for the facts of early Christian history.

of Jesus, which is one of the most astounding miracles of all, then I've opened the door to accepting the historicity of the other miracles as well. If Jesus actually rose from the dead, it isn't hard to imagine that he actually healed the sick, cast out demons, or even walked on liquid H_2O.

I said that the resurrection leads the way to the acceptance of miracles in the Gospels, *however ironically*. What I meant was that, of all the miracles in Matthew, Mark, Luke, and John, the resurrection is the most difficult for many people to accept. Naturalistic scholars have found ways to account for Jesus' healings (psychosomatic or paranormal) and exorcisms (the power of suggestion). But the resurrection cannot be so stripped of its supernatural essence. The once popular view that Jesus didn't really die on the cross, but just "swooned," only to "rise" by awaking in the refreshing coolness of the tomb, has long since been discarded as utterly incredible. So the resurrection leads the way to acceptance of miracles, even though it is the hardest of all miracles to accept if you're not a theist. Nevertheless, once you believe that Jesus in fact rose from the dead, it makes it easier to believe that the Gospel stories about his other miracles have a solid basis in fact and are not just early Christian fiction.

6. It is reasonable to believe that the Gospel miracles actually happened, but this cannot be proved beyond a shadow of a doubt.

I've tried to show that it's reasonable to believe that the miracles of Jesus as portrayed in the canonical Gospels actually happened. The theory that Jesus performed miracles surely helps to account for his widespread influence in his own day. And the notion that he rose from the dead helps to explain the otherwise inexplicable rise of early Christianity. Such theories are reasonable, as I've explained, from the perspective of a theist who believes in a God who can do unusual things in his creation.

Reasonableness and proof are not the same thing, however. There is no way I can prove that Jesus actually did miracles or actually rose from the dead. Nor can anyone prove that he didn't, for that matter. History doesn't allow for such proof, but only for contingent knowledge based on evidence, probabilities, and reasoned argument. So, as a historian of early Christianity, I would argue that it's highly probable that the Gospels faithfully portray the miracles of Jesus as they happened, given, of course, the shaping of tradition and the evangelists' intentions. I would also argue that a theistic approach that allows for miracles produces the most elegant and persuasive account of Jesus' ministry and the rise of early Christianity. Yet historical inquiry can take us only this far along the road of faith. The next steps take us beyond the assurance that history provides, into the realm of Spirit-inspired conviction.

7. The skepticism of many scholars concerning the historicity of the Gospels is rooted in their denial of the possibility of miracles.

I've said that if you're a theist, then you can entertain the possibility that the Gospels accurately portray the miracles of Jesus as they really happened. But if you're not a theist, if you don't believe that there is a God who is active in human affairs and who can, as he wishes, do things contrary to the usual process of nature, then you have an insurmountable problem with the Gospels. Sure, you can account for some of Jesus' so-called miracles by pointing to psychosomatic influence. But at the end of the day, you're stuck with Gospels that narrate events that you don't believe could have happened.

I'm not offended by the scholar who says, "I don't believe in God, and therefore I don't believe in the possibility of miracles, and therefore I don't believe the Gospel accounts are true." In good Humean fashion, this scholar has chosen to believe that something else must account for the miracle stories in the Gospels other than the possibility that Jesus actually did such wonders. Of course I disagree with this scholar's presuppositions and conclusions. But I respect them as reasonable and forthright, given an atheistic presupposition.

I'm much less happy with scholars who don't acknowledge the impact of their functional atheism on their scholarship. While not admitting their core beliefs, they do scholarship with the assumption that God isn't miraculously involved in human affairs. During the last thirty years I've spent hundreds of hours reading scholarly works on Jesus that assume the Gospels are full of pious fictions. Yet few authors admit openly that their bias against the trustworthiness of the Gospels is fundamentally based on their personal belief that miracles don't happen and that therefore the Gospels must be substantially fictional.

Many of these functionally atheistic scholars aren't intending to be deceptive. They operate in an academic culture where such atheism is simply assumed. It doesn't need to be debated or defended. So, for example, when many scholars evaluate the passages in the Gospels where Jesus predicts his death, they naturally and without argument assume that these predictions reflect the creative work of the early church. Why? Because prophecy is out of the picture. It doesn't happen, or if it does, it doesn't belong in historical scholarship.

My plea isn't for all New Testament scholars to become theists, though I wouldn't mind if this were to happen, of course. Rather, I would simply ask for more honesty and self-awareness on the part of all scholars. If you accept the possibility of miracles and therefore see the Gospels as historically accurate, fess up. If you deny the possibility of miracles, and therefore necessarily deny on the basis of your *a priori* assumption that the Gospel accounts could be truthful, say so. Let's all confess our faith more openly.

Readers of biblical scholarship, whether of the academic or the popular variety, need to be keenly aware of the philosophical presuppositions of the scholars. If a scholar approaches the Gospels from a nontheistic perspective, then you will know in advance much of what that person will assume about the Gospels. You can expect a high level of skepticism, because that is what's demanded when the scholar's worldview confronts the data of the Gospels.

I'm convinced that the presence of miracle stories does not undermine the historical reliability of the Gospels for one who is a theist. If you are an atheist, either philosophical or functional, then the miracles in the Gospels do in fact discount the possibility that these writings are historically reliable. Yes, you might find historical reminiscences among the supernatural legends. But your philosophical presuppositions require that many of the Gospel stories, including the all-important resurrection narratives, are pious fiction or mythologized theology, nothing more.

Chapter 12

Do Historical Sources from the Era of the Gospels Support Their Reliability?

When I was in college, my roommate Larry had a friend who played the cello. Sometimes Larry's friend would rehearse in our dorm. I would hear cello music coming from a common room and think, *Wow! That's pretty good!* I never bothered to meet this cello player or to attend any of his concerts, though I heard they were excellent.

Little did I know that Larry's friend would someday be considered the best cello player in the world. Even when he was in college, experts predicted as much, not that I would have cared, really. Looking back, however, I wish that I'd bothered to meet Yo-Yo Ma when I had the chance . . . or at least to listen to more of his music. But when I was in college, cellists were off my radar screen completely.

Similarly, in the first century A.D., Jesus was almost completely off the radar screen of the Roman Empire. Near the end of the century his followers began to stir things up a bit, thus catching the attention of Roman elites. But it wasn't until the second century that people outside of the Christian church began to care about Jesus. Thus it comes as no surprise that he appears rarely in non-Christian sources before the mid-second century. Yet every now and then Jesus does show up in these sources, in ways that are tantalizing.

In the rest of this chapter I am seeking to answer the question, Do historical sources from the era of the Gospels support their reliability? I will break down this question into two sub-questions:

> Do non-Christian writers from the time in which the Gospels were written confirm the reliability of the Gospels?

> When the Gospels refer to people or places that can be identified from other sources, do these sources confirm what we read in the Gospels?

Do non-Christian writers from the time in which the Gospels were written confirm the reliability of the Gospels?

Roman Sources

> The earliest references to Jesus in Roman writers all come from around A.D. 110. The first of these comes from a Roman governor; the other two from historians.

A Letter from Pliny to Trajan

The governor was a man named Gaius Plinius, whom we call Pliny the Younger (to distinguish him from his uncle, Pliny the Elder, a famous naturalist). The younger Pliny served as the Roman governor of Pontus and Bithynia (northern Turkey) from 111–113 A.D. During his tenure he wrote numerous letters, including a letter to the Emperor Trajan[1] asking how he should deal with Christians who were accused of crimes against Rome.

Pliny's letter provides a fascinating glimpse of early Christian belief and behavior, though relatively little information about Jesus himself. Pliny states that Christians will never "curse Christ" and that they meet together each week, during which time they "sing responsively a hymn to Christ as to a god."[2]

Pliny appeared to have no independent knowledge of Jesus apart from what he had learned from Christians. Nevertheless, he documented the fact that they were becoming a problem in his region and that they held Jesus in the highest regard, calling him "Christ" and worshiping him as God.

Suetonius: "Life of Claudius"

Around A.D. 110 the Roman historian Suetonius wrote a history of the Caesars. In his "Life of Claudius" he appears to mention Jesus, though in a peculiar passage. It reads, "Since the Jews constantly made disturbances at the instigation of Chrestus, he expelled them from Rome."[3] Suetonius refers to an act of Claudius in A.D. 49. The name "Chrestus" might refer to Christ, though the correct Latin name for Christ would be "Christus." Most scholars believe that Suetonius (or his source) simply got the vowels confused.

This passage shows how the Romans would have viewed Christians in the middle of the first century A.D.—as Jews who were making trouble because of somebody named Christ. Like Pliny, Suetonius appears to have had no actual knowledge of Jesus. He may even have imagined Christ to have been a rabble-rouser in Rome around A.D. 49.

---

1. This letter is available online at: http://ccat.sas.upenn.edu/jod/texts/pliny.html.

2. Pliny, *Letters* 10.96, trans. William Melmoth, rev. W. M. L. Hutchinson (Loeb, 1915).

3. Suetonius, "Life of Claudius," 25.4, trans. J. C. Rolfe (Loeb, 1913–1914).

Tacitus: *Annals*

In A.D. 109, Tacitus wrote an extensive history of the first-century Roman Empire. In his discussion of the Emperor Nero, who reigned from 54–68 A.D., Tacitus reported that when citizens blamed Nero for the terrible Roman fire in A.D. 64, he decided to deflect criticism by accusing the Christians. Here's Tacitus's description:

> Consequently, to get rid of the report, Nero fastened the guilt and inflicted the most exquisite tortures on a class hated for their abominations, called Christians by the populace. Christus, from whom the name had its origin, suffered the extreme penalty during the reign of Tiberius at the hands of one of our procurators, Pontius Pilatus, and a most mischievous superstition, thus checked for the moment, again broke out not only in Judaea, the first source of the evil, but even in Rome, where all things hideous and shameful from every part of the world find their centre and become popular.[4]

Apart from Tacitus's fascinating appraisal of Christianity as "a most mischievous superstition," he notes that Christ "suffered the extreme penalty" under Pontius Pilate—an obvious reference to Jesus' crucifixion. This does seem to fix the time of Jesus' death and the ultimate responsibility for that death. Tacitus also locates Jesus and the early Christian movement in Judea.

Jewish Sources

The Talmud

Jesus is mentioned occasionally in the Jewish *Talmud*, though often cryptically. Only a few passages appear to mention Jesus directly, and these—no surprise—are negative. For example, in one tractate of the *Talmud* we read that "Jesus the Nazarene

---

4. Tacitus, *Annals* 15.44, trans. Alfred John Church and William Jackson Brodribb. Various online sources.

practiced magic and led Israel astray."[5] The Talmudic passages may preserve some genuine historical traditions about Jesus even though they were penned at least three centuries (or more) after his death.

JOSEPHUS

In the last decades of the first century A.D., the Jewish historian Josephus wrote several treatises on Jewish history. He wrote to build bridges between Rome and the Jews, to explain why their relationship had been so rocky, and to iron out differences between them.

In one passage of his *Jewish Antiquities* Josephus mentioned Jesus indirectly. His focus was on the killing of James, who is identified as "the brother of Jesus, who was called Christ."[6] In this context Josephus had no need to say more about Jesus himself.

The other passage where Josephus appears to mention Jesus is disputed because it comes to us only by way of medieval Christian sources, and these sources seem to have doctored the original text. Josephus is in the process of describing Jewish conditions under Pontius Pilate when we read:

> Now there was about this time Jesus, a wise man, if it be lawful to call him a man; for he was a doer of wonderful works, a teacher of such men as receive the truth with pleasure. He drew over to him both many of the Jews and many of the Gentiles. He was [the] Christ. And when Pilate, at the suggestion of the principal men amongst us, had condemned him to the cross, those that loved him at the first did not forsake him; for he appeared to them alive again the third day; as the divine prophets had foretold these and ten thousand other wonderful things concerning him. And the tribe of Christians, so named from him, are not extinct at this day.[7]

5. *Talmud, b. Sanh.* 107b.
6. Josephus, *Antiquities* 20.9.1. Translation from *The Works of Josephus*, trans. William Whiston. Electronic edition copyright Hendrickson Publishers and OakTree Software.
7. Ibid., 18.3.3.

Given what we know about Josephus's beliefs (he was not a Christian), it's unlikely that this passage, in its current form, comes from his own hand. Many scholars believe that Josephus actually wrote about Jesus in this context, though without the apparent Christian touches.

Given uncertainty about the second passage, I do not want to claim too much about Josephus's knowledge of Jesus. He did know that Jesus "was called Christ." He also seems to have known a bit about Jesus' ministry, and that he was crucified under Pilate.

Like the Roman historian Tacitus, Josephus placed Jesus in Judea, where he was crucified under the authority of Pilate. Both writers, along with Pliny and Suetonius, also testify to the vigor of the early Christian movement. This isn't a lot of information about Jesus, to be sure. But it does confirm what we read in the Gospels. And, curiously enough, it confirms what is absolutely central to the Christian story: the death of Jesus under Pilate. It also hints that something very unusual happened after Jesus' death. Otherwise there's no way to explain why the early Christian movement was so lively that even Rome began to take notice of it.

When the Gospels refer to people or places that can be identified from other sources, do these sources confirm what we read in the Gospels?

Yes, this is certainly true when it comes to the prominent historical landmarks of Jesus' day. When the Gospels identify major leaders, for example, they get the facts right. Jesus was born while Augustus was indeed the Roman emperor (Luke 2:1) and while Herod the Great was king of Judea (Matt. 2:1). Jesus began his ministry during the reign of Tiberius (Luke 3:1). He was crucified when Pontius Pilate was governor of Judea (Mark 15:1) and Herod Antipas was tetrarch of Galilee and Perea (Luke 23:7).

The Gospels also speak accurately about the anonymous people who filled the world of Jesus. It's likely that there would have been a centurion in Capernaum, helping to keep the peace for the sake of Rome (Matt. 8:5). The Pharisees, scribes, and Sadducees are portrayed in the Gospels in a way that fits with what we know about them from other sources. So, for example, when the Pharisees get upset because the followers of Jesus pick grain on the Sabbath (Mark 2:23), this makes historical sense.

The geography of the Gospels is clearly that of first-century Palestine, not some first-century Narnia. Once again, the evangelists put the major landmarks in the right places. When they place Capernaum by the Sea of Galilee, for example, this is correct. And when they refer to Jesus as going "up" to Jerusalem, even though he's traveling south, they get the elevation right, since a trip to Jerusalem involved going up, literally. The vast majority of geographical references in the Gospels fit with what we know from other sources about the region in which Jesus ministered.

I don't mean to whitewash the challenges, however. A few geographical references in the Gospels can seem perplexing, though these can usually be accounted for by a combination of careful exegesis, up-to-date archeology, and an open mind.

For example, Matthew, Mark, and Luke all tell the story of Jesus sending demons out of a man and into a herd of pigs, which then rush into the Sea of Galilee and drown (Matt. 8:28–34; Mark 5:1–20; Luke 8:26–39). Mark and Luke place this event in the country of the Gerasenes, while Matthew describes it as taking place in the land of the Gadarenes. Not only does this seem to be a contradiction among the Gospels, but also the ancient towns we know as Gadara and Gerasa were not close enough to the Sea of Galilee for the event to have taken place nearby. Gadara was about 5 miles from the Sea of Galilee, whereas Gerasa was about 30 miles away. Among the various options for solving this problem are the following:

1. The evangelists weren't precise about the location because geographical precision wasn't demanded of history writing of the first century A.D.

2. The evangelists were speaking of the region *near* Gadara and/or Gerasa, not the towns themselves. We regularly do this sort of thing when we talk about locations. If I meet someone from another state, I'll often say that I live in Orange County, California. If I meet someone from another country, I might say that I live in Los Angeles, even though I really live 50 miles away. Actually, I often say that I live near Disneyland, which almost everybody has heard of. So when people ask where I live, I choose from a variety of answers: Irvine, Orange County, Los Angeles, near Disneyland. All of these are true in a sense.

3. The event happened in another town, known as Khersa, which was on the shore of the Sea of Galilee, and which in Greek would have been spelled in the same way as Gerasa. (I'll say more about this option in the next chapter.)

The case of historical personages is similar to that of geographical references. The Gospels get the main characters right. But once in a while things are not so simple. Consider the case of Quirinius, who was ruling during the time of the census that brought Mary and Joseph to Bethlehem (Luke 2:1–2). Luke refers to a census "taken while Quirinius was governor of Syria" (v. 2). Given the fact that King Herod the Great was reigning when Jesus was born, this census must have taken place around 6 B.C., since Herod died in 4 B.C. (Yes, our calendar is wrong by about 6 years.) But secular sources date Quirinius's term of office to 6–9 A.D., or about ten or fifteen years after the birth of Jesus. Some scholars have seen this as evidence of Luke's inaccuracy as a historian. Yet close attention to the grammar of Luke's claim in verse 2 and awareness of the long political career of Quirinius allow for several ways to view Luke as historically accurate.[8]

---

8. For a detailed and readable discussion of this issue, see Ben Witherington's discussion of the "Birth of Jesus," in *Dictionary of Jesus and the Gospels*, ed. Joel B.

Sure, it would be nicer if Luke had named as governor of Syria P. Quintilius Varus, the Roman legate who supervised in 6 B.C. But if you have done much study of ancient history, you know that apparent confusions like this are frustratingly common. So the tendency of some scholars to rush to judgment against Luke is unwarranted, both in this case and in others like it. When I was in graduate school, some (but not all) of my professors would summarily reject an evangelist's accuracy by saying things like, "Luke is wrong here about Quirinius's governorship" or "Mark has obviously confused the location of Gerasa." Arguments in defense of the Gospel writers' accuracy either were not considered or were quickly rejected as a remnant of naïve fundamentalism. This seemed ironic to me, since these same professors often spent hours in class teasing nuanced meanings out of ancient texts. They were experts at this sort of painstaking exegesis, truly. Yet when it came to the possible historicity of the Gospels, nuance and thoughtful exegesis were often rejected in favor of what could only be called fundamentalist-like literalism: "Luke says it. It's wrong. And that settles it."

If we work hard on understanding what the Gospel writers really meant, and if we allow for the inherent imprecision of ancient records, and if we judge the Gospels by the standards of their own time, then the rare complications within them lose their significance, overshadowed by the extent to which the Gospels agree with secular history. When the biblical Gospels speak of people or places, they undoubtedly get all the major items correct, as well as most of the minor ones. There are some places in which the Gospels seem at first to be less than accurate, but none of these is terribly significant for the author's main purpose, and all of these cases can be interpreted in ways that uphold the historical precision of the evangelists.

Green and Scot McKnight (Downers Grove, Ill.: InterVarsity Press, 1992).

Other First-Century Jewish Sources for Jesus

Josephus wasn't the only Jewish writer in the first century to mention Jesus. Yes, he was the only *non-Christian* Jewish writer to do so. But there were several other Jewish writers who referred to Jesus. These are the authors of the New Testament documents besides the Gospels, several of whom would have considered themselves to be Jews.

The writers of the New Testament, besides the evangelists, were not attempting to write anything like history or biography. But occasionally they referred to Jesus in ways that help to fill in the historical blanks. Perhaps the best illustration comes from 1 Corinthians 15:3–5:

> For I handed on to you as of first importance what I in turn had received: that Christ died for our sins in accordance with the scriptures, and that he was buried, and that he was raised on the third day in accordance with the scriptures, and that he appeared to Cephas, then to the twelve.

Paul wrote this in the early 50s A.D., referring to oral traditions he had received earlier. So we have in this passage historical information that comes from within fifteen or twenty years of Jesus' death. You'll notice that there isn't anything here about Jesus' life. The tradition focuses on that which was believed by the early Christians to be most important for salvation: his death, burial, and resurrection. These events, by the way, were considered most important by the Gospel writers as well.

Paul's tradition did not come from neutral observers. It was formulated by early Christians who believed that Jesus was the Christ (Messiah) and the Savior. So this passage doesn't add to our non-Christian sources for Jesus. But it does reveal some of the earliest historical information about Jesus, information that is external to and prior to the New Testament Gospels.

Notice, as I have mentioned previously with respect to the Gospel writers, that the historical traditions about Jesus were shaped according to the early Christian theological perspective. Jesus died "for our sins in accordance with the scriptures." Similarly, he was raised "in accordance with the scriptures." These are theological statements, to be sure. But, contrary to the assumptions of some scholars, the fact that they are theological does not rule out the fact that they are also statements based on what really happened. This passage from Paul illustrates why history mattered so much to the early Christians. They believed that what actually happened to Jesus—his death, burial, and resurrection—were the locus of God's salvation. If Jesus had not actually been crucified, buried, and raised, then, as Paul said a few verses later in 1 Corinthians, "our proclamation has been in vain and your faith has been in vain" (1 Cor. 15:14).

Summing Up the Sources Outside of the Gospels

Comparing the Gospels to what we know of first-century history and geography suggests that they are historically accurate. They do not place Jesus in some make-believe world filled with make-believe people. Rather, the Gospels locate Jesus sensibly in the midst of Palestine in the first century A.D. This shows that they are generally reliable, though, of course, it doesn't prove that their portraits of Jesus were accurate.

If we didn't have the biblical Gospels, we wouldn't know much about the historical Jesus. From the later, noncanonical Gospels we would be able to glean a few facts, but not nearly as much as we get from the New Testament Gospels. They remain our chief sources of information about Jesus.

However, if we had to piece together the data about Jesus from sources outside of the Gospels—from Roman writers, from Josephus, and from Paul and the other New Testament writers—we would come up with a little. We would have Jesus, a Jew from Judea, who for some reason got in trouble with Pontius Pilate and was crucified. We would also know that something amazing happened after his death because his followers actually multiplied dramatically. For some reason, they believed that Jesus was the Christ, the Jewish Messiah, even though he had done a most "unmessianic" thing in getting himself crucified. This picture of Jesus is sketchy, to be sure, but it focuses on the most important aspects of the Christian Gospel: the death and resurrection of Jesus.

So, the historical sources outside of the Gospels confirm their core content, but not the details. What about archeology? What does this discipline have to offer? I'll answer this question in the next chapter.

Chapter 13

Does Archeology Support the Reliability of the Gospels?

Does archeology support the reliability of the Gospels? The basic answer is yes. The discovery of ancient artifacts, documents, locations, and inscriptions has in many cases confirmed the accuracy of the New Testament Gospels. In fact, sometimes archeology has helped solve some of the perplexing riddles of New Testament interpretation.

There's no way I can even begin to cover the vast topic of archeology in relationship to the Gospels. What I will supply, therefore, are four tiny glimpses of the overall picture. These will help to illustrate ways in which archeology confirms the accuracy of the New Testament.

151

The Synagogue in Capernaum

The Gospels (Mark 1:21) state (or imply) that Jesus taught in a synagogue in the town of Capernaum along the northwest shore of the Sea of Galilee. The ruins of an ancient synagogue have been found in Capernaum (see photo #5, following page 96, but it dates from the fourth century A.D. Yet beneath this synagogue archeologists uncovered the remains of a still earlier synagogue, one that can be dated to the first century. This earlier building is the place where Jesus taught on several occasions.

The Pilate Inscription

In 1961, in Caesarea Maritima, where Pontius Pilate lived, an inscription was found which, among other things, confirms not only the rule of Pilate in Judea but also his preference for the title "Prefect" (see photo #6, following page 96). The inscription isn't complete anymore, but there's little question about what it once said. In Latin it reads:

TIBERIEUM
IUSPILATUS
ECTUSIUDA

The more complete original wording would be:

TIBERIUM
[PONT]IUS PILATUS
[PRAEF]ECTUS IDU[AEA]

Translated, this reads:

TO TIBERIUS
PONTIUS PILATE
PREFECT OF JUDEA

Obviously this was part of an inscription that originally was a dedication to Tiberius Caesar, perhaps in a temple.

The Cliff at El Kursi

In the last chapter I discussed problems related to the location of Jesus' casting out demons from a man into a herd of pigs, which then ran down a cliff into the Sea of Galilee. The Gospels refer to the location of this event as being in the country of the Gerasenes or Gadarenes. Yet both Gerasa and Gadara are far from the Sea of Galilee. Recent investigations have focused on another town, known today as El Kursi. It was called Gergesa or Khersa in ancient times, which would have been spelled like Gerasa in Greek. Importantly, El Kursi sits on the shore of the Sea of Galilee. An ancient church had been built in El Kursi on top of a site that was considered sacred because Jesus had done something important there. Archeologists found evidence of an ancient graveyard nearby (where the demonized man could have been living). Moreover, there is a steep cliff at El Kursi (see photo #7, following page 96), down which the herd of pigs could have run into the Sea of Galilee. Though the jury is still out on this one, it looks as if the event depicted in the Gospels happened, not at Gerasa or Gadara, but at El Kursi. The evangelists referred either to the city itself or to the region in which it was found.

The Pool of Siloam

In John 9, after healing a blind man, Jesus tells him to go and wash in the pool of Siloam (v. 7). For years it was believed that this pool, or at least its original location, had been identified as being in a particular location in Jerusalem. But then, in 2004, some archeologists digging near the supposed pool of Siloam stumbled upon another pool (see photo #8, following page 96). In the plaster of this pool were found coins that established the date of the pool to the years before and after Jesus. There is little question that this is in fact the pool of Siloam, to which Jesus sent the blind man in John 9.[1]

None of the examples I have just described proves anything specific about Jesus, of course. But they all show that when the Gospels refer to places and people, these places and people really existed.

The Most Important Archeological Discoveries of All

I have not overlooked the archeological discoveries that are arguably the most important for the study of the Gospels. I'm referring to the Dead Sea Scrolls and the collection of writings known as the Nag Hammadi Library, because it was found in Nag Hammadi, Egypt.

It is sometimes claimed, not only that the documents from these discoveries are important for the study of the Gospels, but also that they provide historically accurate data about Jesus, data even more reliable than what we find in the New Testament Gospels. The most quotable and well-known "proponent" of this position is Sir Leigh Teabing, the fictional historian of *The Da Vinci Code* whom we "met" in chapter 2. Here's what he has to say about the Dead Sea Scrolls and the Nag Hammadi Library:

> "Fortunately for historians . . . some of the gospels that Constantine attempted to eradicate managed to survive. The Dead Sea Scrolls were found in the 1950s hidden in a cave near Qumran in the Judean desert. And, of course, the Coptic Scrolls in 1945 at Nag Hammadi. In addition to telling the true Grail story, these documents speak of Christ's ministry in very human terms. Of course, the Vatican, in keeping with their tradition of misinformation, tried very hard to suppress the release of these scrolls. And why wouldn't they? The scrolls highlight glaring historical discrepancies and fabrications, clearly confirming that the modern Bible was compiled and edited by men who

1. Hershel Shanks, "The Siloam Pool: Where Jesus Cured the Blind Man," *Biblical Archeology Review*, September/October 2005, 16–23.

possessed a political agenda—to promote the divinity of the man Jesus Christ and use His influence to solidify their own power base."[2]

Well, that certainly lays down the gauntlet, doesn't it? Is Teabing right? Do the documents found at the Dead Sea (actually in eleven caves, beginning in 1947) and at Nag Hammadi (actually codices, not scrolls) in Egypt in fact contain Gospels that "speak of Christ's ministry in very human terms"? Do they "highlight glaring historical discrepancies and fabrications"? And do they "clearly [confirm] that the modern Bible was compiled and edited by men who possessed a political agenda—to promote the divinity of the man Jesus Christ and use His influence to solidify their own power base"?

I'm tempted to save a lot of time and answer all of these questions with a simple no. *The Da Vinci Code*, after all, is a work of fiction. Teabing's "history" of early Christianity is also mostly fictional. The problem is that this information is presented in the novel as if it were the recognized historical truth that sets the backdrop for the fictional aspects of *The Da Vinci Code*. Many readers, unfamiliar with the actual history of early Christianity, have taken Teabing's view as if it were in fact true. So we must deal with the question of whether or not what Teabing says about the Dead Sea Scrolls and the Nag Hammadi Library is, in fact, accurate. Moreover, even when *The Da Vinci Code* is a distant memory, the issues raised by Teabing will continue to be worthy of consideration.

Before I speak directly about the Dead Sea Scrolls and the books found at Nag Hammadi, I want to add a personal word. I spent a large amount of my time in graduate school studying these writings. One of my professors was on the original translation team for the Scrolls, and two of my professors were involved in the translation of the Nag Hammadi texts. In one seminar I was required to read some of the unpublished Dead Sea Scrolls from photographs taken of the originals, which, if

2. Dan Brown, *The Da Vinci Code* (New York: Doubleday, 2003), 234.

nothing else, gave me lots of respect for those who did this for a living. I don't claim to be an expert on the Scrolls or the Nag Hammadi codices, but I'm quite familiar with these documents, and I have spent a lot of time interacting with those who are experts in this material.

Do the Dead Sea Scrolls Undermine the Reliability of the Gospels?

No. In fact they support it. First of all, the Scrolls are Jewish sectarian documents (including substantial portions of the Hebrew Bible) that do not mention Jesus or early Christianity. Yes, I'm aware that a few so-called scholars see Jesus secretly encoded into the Scrolls, but their theories haven't persuaded any serious scholars. So one might be tempted to say that the Dead Sea Scrolls are irrelevant to the question of the Gospels' reliability.

But this would be a mistake. What the Scrolls reveal in great detail is the life and thought of a group of Jews more or less contemporaneous with Jesus and early Christianity. Whether Jesus himself had contact with any of these people is debatable, though many scholars believe they influenced John the Baptist, who then influenced Jesus. Yet even if a connection this obvious didn't exist, the Scrolls help us understand the Jewish world in which Jesus operated. They illustrate the variety of messianic expectations in the time of Jesus. And they show how Jesus' teaching fits nicely within the Jewish world of first-century Palestine.

Let me cite one example. Before the discovery of the Dead Sea Scrolls, it was common in some scholarly quarters to view the teaching of Jesus in the Gospel of John as thoroughly Hellenistic, and therefore unlikely to have come from Jesus himself. But when the Scrolls were discovered, many of the supposedly Greek aspects of Jesus' teaching in John, like the contrast between darkness and light, were seen to be thoroughly at home in the Judaism of Jesus' own day. In this case—and there are many like it—the Scrolls confirm the reliability of the New Testament Gospels in their portrayal of Jesus.

The Dead Sea Scrolls are extraordinarily important for the understanding of Jesus and early Christianity—truly a monumental find. Yet I'm not aware of anything in the Scrolls that undermines the reliability either of the Gospels or of orthodox Christianity. This means, by the way, that nothing in the Scrolls relates to the fictional claims of Leigh Teabing. There are no Gospels among the Scrolls. No "Grail story." No historical discrepancies. And nothing in the Scrolls speaks of Jesus Christ. Yet, insofar as they help us understand his world, they reinforce our confidence in the reliability of the Gospels.

Do the Nag Hammadi Codices Undermine the Reliability of the New Testament Gospels?

Unlike in the case of the Dead Sea Scrolls, Leigh Teabing has a shot at being correct when he talks about the Nag Hammadi Library. The codices from Nag Hammadi do contain a number of so-called Gospels, and these do contain a picture of Jesus which, for the most part, diverges from what we find in the New Testament.

According to Teabing's thesis, the Nag Hammadi documents tell "the true Grail story" and "speak of Christ's ministry in very human terms." In fact they have virtually nothing to say about "the true Grail story" as it's presented in *The Da Vinci Code*. The claim that the Gospels from Nag Hammadi reveal Jesus' secret marriage to Mary Magdalene depends on a misinterpretation of two passages from the library, passages that constitute less than one-tenth of one percent of the whole Nag Hammadi collection.[3]

Moreover, if you were to spend an hour or so perusing the Nag Hammadi Library, you would be surprised by the picture

3. I've examined the Nag Hammadi evidence for the marriage of Jesus in my series *The Da Vinci Opportunity*, http://www.markdroberts.com/htmfiles/resources/davinciopportunity.htm.

of Jesus you would find. Far from presenting a more human Jesus, the Nag Hammadi documents actually portray a much less human Jesus than the one we find in the New Testament Gospels. For the most part, they don't have the slightest interest in the human Jesus. The Nag Hammadi "Christ" or "Savior" comes across as an odd, other-worldly revealer, hardly the fully human being we find in the New Testament. This makes perfect sense, of course, since the Nag Hammadi Library includes many Gnostic documents that deny the value of the flesh and look for a non-fleshly "spiritual" redeemer.

Here are a few passages from some of the Gospels of the Nag Hammadi Library.[4] These illustrate the kind of Jesus found there:

> The Gospel of truth is a joy for those who have received from the Father of truth the gift of knowing him, through the power of the Word that came forth from the pleroma, the one who is in the thought and the mind of the Father, that is, the one who is addressed as "the Savior", (that) being the name of the work he is to perform for the redemption of those who were ignorant of the Father, while the name [of] the Gospel is the proclamation of hope, being discovery for those who search for him (*Gospel of Truth*, 16:31–17:4).

> Jesus said to [Salome], "I am He who exists from the Undivided. I was given some of the things of My father." [Salome said,] "I am Your disciple." [Jesus said to her,] "Therefore I say, if he is undivided, he will be filled with light, but if he is divided, he will be filled with darkness" (*Gospel of Thomas* 61).

> [The Lord said,] "The world came about through a mistake. For he who created it wanted to create it imperishable and immortal. He fell short of attaining his desire. For the world never was imperishable, nor, for that matter, was he who made the world" (*Gospel of Philip* 75:2–9).

4. All translations come from James M. Robinson, ed., *The Nag Hammadi Library in English* (New York: Harper & Row, 1977).

[Mary said,] "What is hidden from you I will proclaim to you." And she began to speak to them these words: "I," she said, "I saw the Lord in a vision and I said to him, 'Lord, I saw you today in a vision.' He answered and said to me, 'Blessed are you that you did not waver at the sight of me. For where the mind is, there is the treasure.' I said to him, 'Lord, how does he who sees the vision see it [through] the soul [or] through the spirit?' The Savior answered and said, 'He does not see through the soul nor through the spirit, but the mind. . . .'" (*Gospel of Mary* 10:7–21)[5].

Lest you think I chose the oddest passages from the Nag Hammadi Library, I would encourage you to read it for yourself. If you really want a wild ride, read portions of *The Thunder, Perfect Mind*, or the *Trimorphic Protennoia*. Then, if you really want to stretch your mind, check out this part of the *Gospel of the Egyptians*:

Domedon Doxomedon came forth, the aeon of the aeons, and the throne which is in him, and the powers which surround him, the glories and the incorruptions. The Father of the great light who came forth from the silence, he is the great Doxomedon-aeon, in which the thrice-male child rests. And the throne of his glory was established in it, this one on which his unrevealable name is inscribed, on the tablet [...] one is the word, the Father of the light of everything, he who came forth from the silence, while he rests in the silence, he whose name is in an invisible symbol. A hidden, invisible mystery came forth: iiiiiiiiiiiiiiiiiiiii EEEEEEEEEEEEEEEEEEEEEE ooooooooooooooooooooo uuuuuuuuuuuuuuuuuuuuu eeeeeeeeeeeeeeeeeeeee aaaaaaaaaaaaaaaaaaaaa OOOOOOOOOOOOOOOOOOOOO (*Gospel of the Egyptians* 43:9–44:9).

After you've spent time actually reading the documents from Nag Hammadi, the notion that they "speak of Christ's min-

5. Note: The *Gospel of Mary* is published in Robinson, ed., *Nag Hammadi Library in English*, though it wasn't found at Nag Hammadi.

istry in very human terms," as claimed by in *The Da Vinci Code* will strike you not only as wrong but as verging on the ridiculous.

Do the Nag Hammadi documents "highlight glaring historical discrepancies and fabrications" when they're compared with the New Testament Gospels? Yes, they do, in a sense. The dominant picture of Jesus in the Nag Hammadi Library differs considerably from the dominant picture of Jesus in the New Testament. If one image is historical, then the other isn't. And if one is authentic, then the other is fabricated. The key question is: Which picture of Jesus is most likely to be the historically accurate one? The obvious answer is: the picture found in the New Testament Gospels.

Why do I say this? First of all, the New Testament Gospels were written within 30 to 70 years after the death of Jesus. The Nag Hammadi Gospels, with the possible exception of *Thomas*, were written at least 100 years after Jesus, with some more than 150 years later. Not only are the New Testament Gospels much older than the Nag Hammadi documents, but also, as I have shown in chapter 5, the New Testament Gospels utilized earlier written sources and public oral traditions. Thus, in the race for historical reliability, the biblical Gospels have lapped the Gnostic Gospels more than once.

Furthermore, the picture of Jesus in the Nag Hammadi Library bears little resemblance to anything that fits within first-century-A.D. Jewish life. Their vision of a Gnostic redeemer reflects the Hellenistic milieu in which the Nag Hammadi Gospels were written. So, any "glaring historical . . . fabrications" will be found, not in the New Testament Gospels, but in the Nag Hammadi Gospels. Thus Teabing's thesis is partly right, in that there are "discrepancies and fabrications," but completely wrong in its estimation of which Gospels are credible and which are fictional.

I don't mean to suggest, however, that the Nag Hammadi Library is not an invaluable find. It allows us to understand Christian Gnosticism with unprecedented insight. But this collection of documents has little to offer to the quest for the historical Jesus, apart from what might be gleaned from the *Gospel of Thomas* and a few other passages in the Nag Hammadi Library that may be traceable through oral traditions back to Jesus himself.

Summing Up

In summary, nothing in the Dead Sea Scrolls or the Nag Hammadi Library undermines the reliability of the biblical Gospels. In fact, the opposite is true. The Dead Sea Scrolls help us understand the world of Jesus, and they illustrate how well the Jesus of the New Testament Gospels fits within that world, in contrast to the Jesus of the noncanonical Gospels. Comparing the "Christ" found in the Nag Hammadi Library with the Jesus found in the New Testament underscores the realism of the biblical Gospels and their portrayal of a truly human, Jewish Jesus, unlike the other-worldly Redeemer of the Gnostic Gospels.

There is one part of Teabing's case against the biblical Gospels that I haven't yet considered. He claims that "the modern Bible was compiled and edited by men who possessed a political agenda—to promote the divinity of the man Jesus Christ and use His influence to solidify their own power base."[6] Is this true? Did the political agenda of the early church influence the writing, editing, and selection of the Gospels for the sake of the power of the orthodox church? This is the topic of the next chapter.

6. Brown, *Da Vinci Code*, 234.

Chapter 14

Did the Political Agenda of the Early Church Influence the Content of the Gospels?

I ended the last chapter by quoting from *The Da Vinci Code*'s fictional Sir Leigh Teabing, who said, "the modern Bible was compiled and edited by men who possessed a political agenda—to promote the divinity of the man Jesus Christ and use His influence to solidify their own power base."[1] In the next chapter I'll take up the question of how and why Matthew, Mark, Luke, and John made it into the canon of Scripture—what Teabing might have called the "power base" of early Christian leaders. In this chapter I want to focus on the "edited by men who possessed a political agenda" part of Teabing's claim.

"It's All about Power"

Dan Brown, author of *The Da Vinci Code*, didn't make up the "political agenda" charge out of thin air. In this postmodern

1. Dan Brown, *The Da Vinci Code* (New York: Doubleday, 2003), 234.

age, everybody supposedly has an "agenda," and almost always this agenda has something to do with power. People don't believe what they do because they think it's true but because it undergirds their power, or so the story goes. A postmodern critic might write off this book, for example, not because my ideas are faulty but because I'm simply trying to augment my personal and professional power by defending the Gospels. The reliability of the Gospels, it might be argued, props up my pastoral power, or helps me sell books, or whatever.

If you do much reading by scholars who are enamored with Gnosticism, you'll find an argument similar to that of Leigh Teabing. The orthodox church was in a battle with the Gnostics, a battle for power, these scholars will say. Everything the orthodox leaders did, like write treatises against heresies, was for the purpose of protecting and extending their power. In the end, the strong defeated the weak, and Gnosticism disappeared, at least for the most part.

When it comes to the New Testament Gospels, therefore, it is argued that they were chosen and edited as part of the orthodox power grab. Matthew, Mark, Luke, and John won out, not because of their truthfulness but because of their usefulness. They helped promote the orthodox Christian agenda: to dominate other Christian groups and to augment ecclesiastical power in the Roman Empire.

In this chapter I will evaluate the power-grab theory. But before doing so, I want to consider a related question that will help us understand the motivations of the early Christians: Does the content of the Gospels reflect the theological agenda of the early church?

The Gospels and the Early Christian Theological Agenda

Orthodox Christians in the first and second centuries believed some astounding things about Jesus. They believed that he was, not only the ultimate purveyor of God's wisdom, but divine Wisdom in the flesh. They affirmed that Jesus was the Messiah of Israel, the one who had begun to inaugurate the kingdom of God on earth. They even went so far as to confess Jesus as Lord, as the man who was also Emmanuel, God with us.

The first Christians didn't just believe these things. They went around trying to get everybody else to believe them too. The first post-Easter followers of Jesus focused their efforts upon their fellow Jews. But before long, Christians were promoting Jesus to Gentiles throughout the Roman world, and finding considerable success in doing so.

One would expect, therefore, as Leigh Teabing claims, that the biblical Gospels should highlight the divinity of Jesus and downplay his humanity. Yet this expectation turns out to be misguided. Oh, to be sure, the deity of Jesus can be found in the Gospels, especially in John. But his humanity takes center stage. And his claims to divinity are usually veiled, suggestive more than didactic. Given what the early Christians believed about Jesus, if they were making up sayings by him and doctoring the Gospels to suit their agendas, you would expect to find lots of "I am God" sayings. Yet this is one thing Jesus never explicitly says. It's there, to be sure, but only between the lines.[2]

The canonical Gospels portray Jesus as a real person. Though miraculously conceived, he was born in the ordinary way. He experienced such genuinely human realities as anger (Mark 3:5), exhaustion (John 4:6), compassion (Mark 6:34), impatience (Mark 9:19), love (Mark 10:21), weeping (John 11:35), joy (Luke 10:21), grief (Mark 14:34), thirst (John 19:28), and uncertainty about his divine calling (Mark 14:36). Jesus touched lepers (Matt. 8:3), ate with notorious sinners (Mark 2:16), and embraced children (Mark 10:16). When he was beaten and crucified, the Jesus of the biblical Gospels spilled real blood and felt real pain. To be sure, Jesus did and said

---

2. In the Gospel of John, Jesus comes the closest to saying that he is God (see, for example, 8:58; 10:30; 14:9). But even here he never quite says, "I am God," though this implication is clear.

unusual things. But Matthew, Mark, Luke, and John paint a truly human Jesus, yet one who is also the Son of God.

The Gospels also present aspects of Jesus' life and ministry that, it would seem, editors bent on emphasizing his divinity would have minimized or eliminated. Sometimes, for example, Jesus appears not to be omniscient, as when he asked, "Who touched me?" (Luke 8:45) or when he admitted that he didn't know the time of his return (Mark 13:32). In other cases his healing powers seem oddly limited (Mark 6:1–6). And then there's the stirring picture of Jesus in Gethsemane, which, though moving for Christians, doesn't exactly portray Jesus as an impressive god (Mark 14:32–42). Finally, of course, there's the utterly scandalous presentation of Jesus' crucifixion, which was a massive stumbling block to acceptance of Jesus as divine in the Hellenistic world. Yet the biblical Gospels resolutely held on to the scandal of the cross.

This stands in stark contrast to the Jesus, or more often the "Christ" or "Savior," of the noncanonical Gospels. There he is a superman who reveals esoteric truth and doesn't involve himself with things like true humanity or crucifixion. If you're looking for a human Jesus, check out Matthew, Mark, Luke, and John. If you want an otherworldly redeemer, stick with the Gnostic Gospels.

The most central affirmation of the earliest Christians was that Jesus was the Messiah, the Christ. This is indeed striking since he did not fulfill typical Jewish expectations for the Messiah by reestablishing the kingdom of Israel and vanquishing the Roman oppressors. It's even more surprising given the fact that Jesus died on a Roman cross, a victim of Roman imperial power. Yet, as the first Christians sorted out the meaning of Jesus in light of his life, teaching, death, and resurrection, they came to believe that he was, indeed, God's Messiah. So central was this belief that before long "Christ" (meaning "Messiah" in Greek) became a substitute for Jesus' name.

So, given the centrality of Christian belief in Jesus as the Messiah, and especially given the tension between this belief and Jewish expectations, you might expect the Gospels to be full of sayings of Jesus that make crystal clear both the fact and the nature of his messiahship. Yet, once again, this expectation leads to a dead end. In surprisingly few places in the Gospels other people say that Jesus is the Messiah. Yet he never does. Only once does Jesus clearly admit to being the Messiah (Mark 14:62), but even then he quickly changes the subject and starts talking about the "Son of Man." I'm not arguing that Jesus was not the Messiah, or that this identification can't be derived from the Gospels. Indeed, it can be. I'm merely pointing out that if the content of the Gospels had been driven by the early Christian theological agenda, you would expect to find much more about Jesus as Messiah. The absence of such sayings shows that those who passed on the traditions about Jesus orally, and those who wrote them down, did not in fact let their agenda spill over into their memories of Jesus.

I've said earlier that the evangelists wrote in light of their agendas—to teach, convert, defend, or whatever. Like other Hellenistic biographers, they narrated events from the life of Jesus in order to influence the lives of their readers. But the actual contents of the Gospels are surprisingly free of the kind of agenda-driven material we might expect from people who played fast and loose with the truth. In fact, the evangelists and their sources, both oral and written, were highly commit-ted to the truth of what Jesus did and said, even when it was inconvenient.

The Gospels and Orthodox Ecclesiastical Power

I've shown that the New Testament Gospels include material that doesn't fit very well with the early Christian theological agenda. But what about the desire for power? Do the Gospels provide a solid foundation for the power of the orthodox church?

According to a common thesis popularized in *The Da Vinci Code*, the writing, editing, and collecting of the New Testament Gospels was primarily about power. All of this reflected the effort of the orthodox church to establish power, especially over rival heretical groups like the Gnostics.

There was indeed a power struggle within Christendom in the second and third centuries. And the orthodox church did indeed claim, among other things, the power to teach the truth about the ministry and nature of Jesus. One of the church's key arguments was that their sacred writings, their ecclesiastical leaders, and their basic beliefs were *apostolic* in origin. The writings were either written by the first disciples of Jesus (including Paul) or by their associates, and were consistent with apostolic teaching. The bishops could trace their authority back to the earliest disciples of Jesus, so their leadership was also apostolic. Church power was derived from Jesus, of course, through the mediation of the apostles.

Given the centrality of the apostles, especially the first disciples of Jesus, in the church's claim to rightful authority, it is fascinating and telling to note how the disciples of Jesus are actually portrayed in the New Testament Gospels. They are, after all, the first leaders of the church. They are the ones from whom the church drew its power. Yet they are the ones whom the Gospels portray as . . . well . . . faithless, foolish, and unreliable. Not exactly what you would expect from Gospels that were written and edited to undergird the power of the orthodox church!

In the Gospels, the disciples of Jesus are first seen in a positive light, as they leave their familiar lives behind to follow Jesus (Mark 1:16–20). But things go downhill quickly from there. For example:

- The disciples consistently misunderstand Jesus (e.g., Matt. 16:5–12; Mark 10:13–14, 35–40; John 12:1–7).
- They are self-seeking, concerned for their own greatness and glory (e.g., Mark 9:34; 10:35–37).
- They lack faith in God or Jesus (e.g., Matt. 8:26; Matt. 14:31).

- They are rebuked by Jesus for being people "of little faith" (Matt. 8:26). Worse still, Jesus once expresses his exasperation over the disciples: "You faithless and perverse generation, how much longer must I be with you?" (Matt. 17:17).

- They abandon Jesus in his hour of greatest need, sleeping while he asks them to join him in prayer at Gethsemane (Mark 14:32–43). Then, when he is arrested, all of them desert Jesus and run away to save their own necks (Mark 14:50). None of the male disciples is present at the cross, except for "the disciple whom Jesus loved" (John 21:20).

- After the resurrection, the disciples disbelieve Mary's report that Jesus is risen (Luke 24:11) and some doubt (or are hesitant) even when they see the risen Christ (Matt. 28:17).

If you read through the four biblical Gospels, you'll find that the disciples are almost never pictured as paragons of faith or wisdom. Time and again they're portrayed negatively. This fact, all by itself, seems to me to disprove the power-grab thesis. If writers, editors, and collectors of the Gospels had been motivated by a desire for power, surely they would have cleaned up the Gospel record. The portrayal of the disciples in the Gospels strongly suggests that the early Christian tradition and the four evangelists were willing to pass on the truth even if that truth portrayed their founding leaders in an embarrassing light.

The Gospels and the First "Pope"

Ecclesiastical authority in the first centuries after Christ was based on a connection between church leaders and the original apostles. Increasingly, however, Peter began to play a leading role in the ecclesiastical scenario. He was, after all, the "rock" upon which Jesus promised to build his church (Matt. 16:18).

169

And he was believed to be the first bishop of the Roman church, that is, the first pope.

So how does Peter fare in the New Testament Gospels? Worse than the rest of the disciples! He's outstanding for his foibles, especially in crucial moments of Jesus' ministry. Let me cite a few examples:

- In Matthew 14:22–33, the disciples of Jesus are in a boat on the Sea of Galilee. Jesus comes to them from the shore, walking on the water. Peter gets out of the boat in order to approach Jesus. An exemplar of faith? Hardly! He becomes frightened and starts to sink, crying out to be saved. Jesus refers to him as one with "little faith."

- Though Peter rightly confesses Jesus as the Messiah (Mark 8:27–33), he doesn't really understand what he's saying. So when Jesus reveals the necessity of his death, Peter actually rebukes him. Jesus responds to Peter by saying, "Get behind me, Satan! For you are setting your mind not on divine things but on human things" (Mark 8:32–33).

- Peter doubly misunderstands the point of Jesus' footwashing, both in not wanting it and then in wanting too much of it (John 13:5–10).

- Peter is obviously special to Jesus since Jesus takes him along to the Garden of Gethsemane. But then Peter, along with two other disciples, keeps falling asleep rather than staying awake in Jesus' hour of turmoil. This is deeply distressing to Jesus (Mark 14:32–42).

- When the guards come to arrest Jesus in the Garden, Peter draws a sword and cuts off the ear of a slave of the high priest, but Jesus rebukes Peter and heals the slave's ear. Clearly Peter doesn't understand Jesus' intentions. He looks impulsive and foolish (John 18:10).

- Peter, along with the rest of the disciples, runs away when Jesus is arrested (Mark 14:50).

170

- Though he vigorously rejected Jesus' prediction that he would deny Jesus, in fact Peter denies Jesus three times (Mark 14:30–31, 66–72).

If you haven't read through the biblical Gospels recently, you might think I've picked only those passages about Peter that show him in a poor light, while ignoring the ones that show him as a strong, wise leader, the kind of leader upon whom Jesus would build the Roman Catholic Church. In the Acts of the Apostles Peter emerges as this sort of leader, but only because the Holy Spirit fills him with power. The Gospels don't paint a flattering portrait of Peter at all.

Can you imagine a movement that allowed such stories of a prominent founder to be told, even to be enshrined in its foundational documents? Usually a movement would make every effort to cover up the failings of its first leaders, to rewrite history in a more flattering way. For example, the official web site of the Mormon Church includes a historical summary of the life of its founder, Joseph Smith.[3] In this summary it is mentioned that Smith married Emma Hale on January 18, 1827. It is not mentioned, however, that Emma was the first of many wives of Joseph Smith, who believed that God had commanded the practice of plural marriage. This is neatly left off of the Joseph Smith page, for very understandable reasons.[4]

The presentation of Peter in the New Testament Gospels shows the folly of the "power grab" theory of Gospel production and authentication. It also shows something quite astounding about early Christian oral tradition and the writing of the Gospels. Those who passed on and wrote down

3. http://www.lds.org/churchhistory/presidents/controllers/potcController .jsp?leader=1&topic=events.
4. The web site does still contain, however, section 132 of the Doctrine and Covenants, in which God purportedly reveals to Joseph Smith his commandment for men to have multiple wives (http://scriptures.lds.org/dc/132). And in a Frequently Asked Questions section it is acknowledged that Joseph Smith obeyed God's command to practice plural marriage (http://www.mormon.org/question/faq/category/answer/0,9777,1601-1-114-1,00.html). But none of this shows up in the biographical material on Smith.

the actions and sayings of Jesus were committed to telling the truth, even when this truth was embarrassing to some of the most prominent leaders of the early church. Surely it was only a strong commitment to historical accuracy that kept such a negative portrayal of the disciples, including Peter, in the New Testament Gospels.

But what about the selection of the Gospels? Was it a quest for power that motivated the orthodox church to recognize Matthew, Mark, Luke, and John while rejecting the other Gospels? Who determined which books made it into the Christian canon, and on what basis? To these questions we shall turn in the next chapter.

Chapter 15

Why Do We Have Only
Four Gospels in the Bible?

In chapter 8, I explained how the fact that we have four different Gospels in the New Testament increases our confidence in their reliability. But one might wonder, why are these four in the Bible? And why only these, given the existence of two or three dozen Gospels among early Christian writings? Who decided that there should be only four biblical Gospels, and on what grounds?

For one last time I turn to Sir Leigh Teabing, *The Da Vinci Code*'s principal historian. He explains quite clearly who chose the biblical Gospels: the Roman emperor Constantine. Teabing also reveals what motivated Constantine to choose Matthew, Mark, Luke, and John: these writings augmented his power because they emphasized the divinity of Jesus, unlike the Gospels rejected by Constantine.[1]

In the last chapter I showed that Teabing's estimation of the biblical Gospels is sorely lacking. He completely reverses the

---

1. Dan Brown, *The Da Vinci Code* (New York: Doubleday, 2003), 231–234.

facts concerning which Gospels portray the most human Jesus. But what about his history of the canon? Did Constantine form the Christian canon? Did he decide which Gospels would be included? Or did all of this happen in another way? No doubt you've guessed that I'll opt for "another way," though I will explain how Constantine may have had a hand in the formation of the Christian Bible.

The question of why we have only four Gospels in the Bible opens up a much larger can of worms: the history of the Christian canon. The English word *canon* comes from the Greek *kanon*, which meant "rule" or "standard." Literally, a *kanon* was something in the toolbox of a Greek carpenter. We would call it a ruler or straightedge. Metaphorically, a *kanon* was a standard for behavior.[2] When Christians first started using the word *kanon* in reference to matters of faith, they referred to their core beliefs, or "rule of faith" as it was often called. In time, however, *kanon* came to describe the official collection of inspired books, the contents of the Bible.

The history of the biblical canon is not a simple topic. How and why the followers of Jesus came to regard both the Old Testament and the New Testament as holy Scripture is a story I can't tell in one short chapter. If you're looking for the longer narrative, check out the books by F. F. Bruce or Bruce M. Metzger.[3] Yet in relatively few words I will explain why, in particular, the early Christians came to regard Matthew, Mark, Luke, and John as so special that they ended up in the Bible.

The Jewish Foundation

The earliest followers of Jesus were Jews. Thus they were familiar with the notion of sacred writings. All Jews in the

2. Henry Liddell and Robert Scott, *A Greek-English Lexicon* (Oxford: Clarendon, 1996), s.v. *kanon*.

3. F. F. Bruce, *The Canon of Scripture* (Downers Grove, Ill.: InterVarsity Press, 1988); Bruce M. Metzger, *The Canon of the New Testament: Its Origin, Development, and Significance* (New York: Oxford University Press, 1997).

first century A.D. considered the Torah, the first five books of our Bible, to be inspired by God and thus authoritative. Many Jews regarded other books as having holy status, including the rest of the books in our Old Testament. Josephus, the Jewish historian, wrote near the end of the first century:

> For we have not an innumerable multitude of books among us, disagreeing from and contradicting one another [as the Greeks have], but only twenty-two books, which contain the records of all the past times; which are justly believed to be divine; and of them five belong to Moses, which contain his laws and the traditions of the origin of mankind till his death, . . . the prophets, who were after Moses, wrote down what was done in their times in thirteen books. The remaining four books contain hymns to God, and precepts for the conduct of human life.[4]

Although not every Jew in the first century would have identified exactly the same books as Scripture, the notion of a collection of authoritative writings was firmly entrenched in the Jewish mind. Thus the early Christians inherited both a high regard for the Jewish Scriptures and the idea that God makes his will known through an authorized set of writings. Here is the ideological and practical background for the Christian canon.

The Authority of Jesus

Jesus regarded the Jewish Scriptures as authoritative, quoting them as God's Word. But he muddied the waters by speaking with such personal authority that he sounded very much like the Scripture itself. One of the qualities that Jesus' Jewish audience found so striking was that he "taught them as one having authority, and not as the scribes" (Mark 1:22). Jesus didn't even bother to imitate the prophets by prefacing his

---

4. Josephus, *Against Apion* 1.38–40. Josephus counts only twenty-two books in part because he counts 1 and 2 Samuel and the like as only one book.

remarks with "Thus saith the Lord." Rather, he simply spoke as if, well, he *were* the Lord.

The early followers of Jesus regarded him as the ultimate authority. Thus they adopted his own use of the Jewish Scriptures, treating them as divinely inspired. This is made clear in a passage from the New Testament:

> All scripture is inspired by God and is useful for teaching, for reproof, for correction, and for training in righteousness, so that everyone who belongs to God may be proficient, equipped for every good work (2 Tim. 3:16–17).

The "scripture" referred to here is what we would call the Old Testament. Only later, by implication, would this verse be understood to relate to the New Testament as well.

Because Jesus was the ultimate authority, the early Christians came to see his words as equal to the Old Testament Scriptures. Jesus spoke the Word of God, even as he was the Word of God incarnate. Thus, once the teachings of Jesus were written down, it was a natural step for Christians to regard these writings as inspired and to use them alongside the Old Testament. We see an example of this in a description of Christian worship in the *First Apology* of Justin Martyr, which was written near the middle of the second century:

> And on the day called Sunday, all who live in cities or in the country gather together to one place, and the memoirs of the apostles or the writings of the prophets are read, as long as time permits; then, when the reader has ceased, the president verbally instructs, and exhorts to the imitation of these good things.[5]

The "memoirs of the apostles," which Justin elsewhere refers to as Gospels,[6] were, by the mid-second century, being used in Christian worship as holy Scripture.

5. Justin Martyr, *First Apology* 67. The translation is from Alexander Roberts and James Donaldson in *The Ante-Nicene Fathers*, reprint ed. (Grand Rapids, Mich.: Eerdmans, 1978–1980).
6. Ibid., 66.

The Fourfold Gospel

At about this same time, orthodox Christians recognized the "fourfold Gospel," the Gospel that came according to Matthew, according to Mark, according to Luke, and according to John. As we have seen earlier, a second-century Christian leader named Tatian—who happened to be a disciple of Justin, by the way—took the four recognized Gospels and harmonized them into one, the *Diatessaron* (a Greek word meaning "out of four").

Though this singular Gospel was popular in Syria, most of the church continued to use the four Gospels rather than Tatian's harmony. The list of authoritative writings known as the Muratorian Canon, which was composed around A.D. 170, referred to four Gospels, mentioning Luke and John by name. It is virtually certain that the other two Gospels were Matthew and Mark. So both Tatian and the author of the Muratorian Canon, along with other writers in the late second century, recognized four Gospels as uniquely authoritative.

The Challenge of the Heretics

Irenaeus was one of these other writers. In his massive refutation of so-called Christians whom he considered to be heretics, Irenaeus referred to the four Gospels as "Scriptures" that are "the ground and pillar of our faith."[7] He recognized that others accepted either more Gospels or fewer Gospels, and he accused them of being "vain, unlearned, and also audacious" for doing so.[8]

Irenaeus specifically mentioned examples of those who recognized something other than four and only four Gospels. Included in these examples is Marcion, who "rejecting the entire Gospel, yea rather, cutting himself off from the Gospel, boasts that he has part in the [blessings of] the Gospel." The

---

7. Irenaeus, *Against Heresies* 3.1.1–2.
8. Ibid., 3.11.9.

followers of Valentinus, on the contrary, "while they put forth their own compositions, boast that they possess more Gospels than there really are." In particular, they upheld the authority of the "Gospel of Truth," a Gospel that may be the same as the document with that name in the Nag Hammadi Library. So some heretics had fewer than four Gospels, while others had more. Neither option, according to Irenaeus, was acceptable.

In fact Marcion did hold on to a piece of the fourfold Gospel, a revised version of Luke, from which Marcion excised everything positive about the Old Testament God, whom Marcion considered to be different from the God of Jesus and opposed to genuine Christianity. Marcion's collection of approved writings also contained tidied-up versions of the letters of Paul.

It is often said that Marcion was the first Christian to have a canon of scripture, albeit a truncated and heretical one. It is also claimed that the notion of a canon came from Marcion. The first claim may be true, though we can't prove it either way. The second claim exaggerates the role of Marcion. As I explained above, the seeds of canonical thought were already planted in the early church by Judaism, Jesus, and the practices of the first believers.

Yet the example of Irenaeus reveals that Marcion did require the orthodox believers to begin to lay out and defend their implicit sense of the canon of Scripture. From Marcion, the church was challenged to account for why it had four Gospels. And from the Gnostic side of things, the church had to explain why only four Gospels were acceptable.

The Development of the Canon

Beginning in the late second century, orthodox Christians began to make official lists of recognized sacred texts. They didn't believe they were making things up so much as recording what the orthodox church already had implicitly affirmed through its use of these texts.

In almost every quarter of the orthodox church, the four Gospels were accepted as canonical. Occasionally some Christians would use other Gospels as well. But the four were uniquely regarded. Debates about which documents belonged in Scripture were common in the third and fourth centuries, though these didn't pertain to the Gospels so much as to other writings, like 3 John or Revelation.

Early in the fourth century A.D. the church historian Eusebius described the writings that were considered to be sacred.[9] He organized them in categories: the accepted writings, the disputed writings, the rejected writings, and the unworthy-of-mention writings. The last category included heretical documents like the *Gospel of Peter* and the *Gospel of Thomas* which, according to Eusebius, "no one belonging to the succession of ecclesiastical writers has deemed worthy of mention in his writings." For our purposes, it is important to note that Eusebius began his list of the accepted writings with "the holy quaternion [set of four] of the Gospels." Beyond this, he includes only books found today in our New Testament. The disputed writings include James, Jude, 2 Peter, 2 John, and 3 John. Revelation seems to fall in two categories: accepted (by some) and rejected (by others).

The first Christian to publish a list of authoritative writings that contained all of the twenty-seven books in our New Testament and only these books was Athanasius, Bishop of Alexandria. In A.D. 367 he wrote a letter to other church leaders in which he listed as sacred books all and only those that now form the New Testament. In this letter Athanasius mentioned the heretics, showing that he, like those who had gone before him, saw the canon of Scripture as a necessary antidote to non-orthodox Christianity:

[N]or is there in any place a mention of apocryphal writings. But they are an invention of heretics, who write them when they choose, bestowing upon them their approbation, and assigning to them a date, that so, using them as ancient writings, they may find occasion to lead astray the simple.[10]

9. Eusebius, *Church History* 3.3.1–7.
10. Athanasius, *Festal Letter for Easter 367* A.D. The translation is from Philip Schaff and Henry Wace, eds., *A Select Library of Nicene and Post-Nicene Fathers*, 2nd series (Grand Rapids, Mich.: Eerdmans, 1978–1979).

The Role of Constantine

By now it should be obvious that Constantine had nothing to do with the recognition of Matthew, Mark, Luke, and John as sacred writings. This happened well over a century before the early years of the fourth century A.D., when Constantine became the Roman emperor. Yet Constantine may have had a role in the development of the canon. It may have been his fondness for the Book of Revelation that encouraged Eusebius to include it among the accepted books.[11]

More importantly, Constantine's desire to bring unity to Christianity may have encouraged the bishops to define with greater precision than before the official list of inspired writings. In fact, Constantine instructed Eusebius to oversee the production of fifty high-quality volumes of "the sacred Scriptures."[12] This would have required a decision about exactly which books to include, and this choice would have been influential throughout the church.

Standards for Inclusion in the Canon

By the fourth century, almost all of the books in our current New Testament were regarded as Scripture. There was no doubt about which Gospels were in and which were out. As we look back upon the process that led to the identification of the canon, we can see the standards used by orthodox church leaders in their determinations.

One of these standards was *antiquity*. For a book to be considered for the canon, it needed to have been around for a long time, and its antiquity must have been part of the public record. The Gnostics were coming up with all sorts of new writings, claiming that they had been composed a long time ago but lacking any means to prove this.

11. Lee M. McDonald, *The Formation of the Christian Biblical Canon: Revised and Expanded Edition* (Peabody, Mass.: Hendrickson, 1995), 188–189.
12. Eusebius, *Life of Constantine* 4.36.

Another standard for canonical consideration was *widespread usage*. If a book was well known throughout the Roman world and was used in many churches, then it stood a much better chance of being regarded as canonical than a book that was used only in certain regions. Moreover, if a book was used in influential churches, such as those in Rome or Alexandria, then this was a strong point in its favor.[13] Again, this standard counted heavily against many of the so-called Gospels that were not widely known and were not used in leading churches.

Two of the most important standards for canonical inclusion can be found in two paragraphs from *Against Heresies* by Irenaeus. In the first paragraph he identified Matthew, Mark, Luke, and John as those who were empowered by the Holy Spirit to pass down the good news. Then he continued:

> These have all declared to us that there is one God, Creator of heaven and earth, announced by the law and the prophets; and one Christ the Son of God. If any one do not agree to these truths, he despises the companions of the Lord; nay more, he despises Christ Himself the Lord; yea, he despises the Father also, and stands self-condemned, resisting and opposing his own salvation, as is the case with all heretics.[14]

Irenaeus shows that canonical documents are *apostolic*. They have a direct connection with the apostles, the first followers of Jesus. This means, in practice, that scriptural books must be written either by apostles, as in the case of Paul's letters and, perhaps, Matthew and John, or by people closely associated with the apostles, like Mark and Luke. Apostolicity also has to do with consistency of content with the original teaching of the apostles. Thus something could be considered apostolic if it were known to be old and if its content was consistent with apostolic preaching.

13. McDonald, *Formation of the Christian Biblical Canon*, 246–249.
14. Irenaeus, *Against Heresies* 3.1.2.

It is easy to see why apostolicity was such a big deal. The apostles were, after all, "the companions of the Lord." They knew Jesus' teaching and had observed his life. Even if they didn't quite get it before his death and resurrection, after these events they not only knew the truth but also were filled with the Spirit so that they might faithfully spread the good news. An apostolic stamp of approval, therefore, was tantamount to an endorsement by Jesus.

The Gnostics also valued apostolicity, which accounts for why they claimed to have Gospels by people like Thomas, Philip, Judas, and Mary Magdalene, not to mention secret writings by James, John, and Peter. Understandably, this presented a tough challenge for the orthodox leaders. They claimed a connection to Jesus through the apostles. So did the Gnostics. Who was right?

Irenaeus illustrates the most effective orthodox response to this question. Of the four Gospels he states, "These have all declared to us that there is one God, Creator of heaven and earth, announced by the law and the prophets; and one Christ the Son of God." The authorized Gospels, unlike the heretical ones, all affirm the same basic truth. This truth is not found in the heretical Gospels, so they must not be valid. At one point Irenaeus shows why the *Gospel of Truth*, embraced by the followers of Valentinus, is not trustworthy:

> Indeed, they have arrived at such a pitch of audacity, as to entitle their comparatively recent writing "the Gospel of Truth," though it agrees in nothing with the Gospels of the Apostles, so that they have really no Gospel which is not full of blasphemy. For if what they have published is the Gospel of truth, and yet is totally unlike those which have been handed down to us from the apostles, . . .[15]

How can we know that the *Gospel of Truth* is "really no Gospel"? Because its essential content differs from the essential content of the apostolic Gospels. Irenaeus used the Greek

15. Ibid., 3.11.9.

word *kanon* to refer to this essential content, which he called "the rule [*kanon*] of truth." Though never fully codified in the second century, as in later creeds, the rule of truth was the core of Christian belief.

The Example of Serapion and the Gospel of Peter

An example from Eusebius illustrates early Christian usage of the Gospels and how they were evaluated by orthodox leaders who applied the *kanon* of truth. The situation concerned the *Gospel of Peter*, a document that was popular among Christians in the second century, many of whom believed it to have been written by Peter himself.

At that time, Serapion, bishop of Antioch, discovered that one of his churches was reading the *Gospel of Peter*. At first, because he believed the church to be orthodox, Serapion didn't bother. But when he studied the text of the *Gospel of Peter* carefully, he discovered that, though it included "many things in accordance with the true doctrine of the Saviour," the *Gospel of Peter* presented Jesus in a heretical way.[16] In particular, he was portrayed as less than fully human. So, on the basis of the inconsistency between the theology of the *Gospel of Peter* and orthodox theology, Serapion rejected this Gospel as inauthentic and not worthy of reading. Curiously, a portion of this Gospel was discovered in the nineteenth century, and it was found to minimize the humanity of Jesus. For example, he is silent on the cross "as though he felt no pain."[17]

Summing Up

Why do we have only four Gospels in the Bible?

16. Eusebius, *Church History* 6.12.6.
17. *Gospel of Peter* 10, trans. Chr. Maurer, in *New Testament Apocrypha, Volume 1: Gospels and Related Writings*, ed. Wilhelm Schneemelcher, Eng. trans. R. McL. Wilson (Philadelphia: Westminster, 1963).

- Because only four Gospels were judged by the early church leaders to be demonstrably old, and thus closely connected to Jesus.
- Because only four Gospels were used throughout the church, especially in leading churches like Rome and Alexandria.
- Because only four Gospels were judged to be truly apostolic, in that they were written either by apostles or by those closely associated with them, and in that they alone accurately embodied the teaching of the apostles.
- Because only four Gospels faithfully represented the "rule of truth," the core of Christian teaching. Consistency with this theological *kanon* led to inclusion in what later became known as the *canon* of sacred writings.

Before the end of the second century, orthodox Christians had used these standards to identify Matthew, Mark, Luke, and John as the Gospels that were truly inspired by God and were thus worthy to be considered as Scripture alongside the writings of the Old Testament.

Contemporary Christians who accept the canon don't do so because they believe that nothing of value can be found in the noncanonical writings. Many of these writings, such as those known as the Apostolic Fathers, are both orthodox and inspirational. But they are not included in the canon because they fall short in one or more ways.

Even the unorthodox noncanonical writings are worth reading, at least by those who want to understand early church history. The Nag Hammadi documents, for example, contain a wealth of information about Gnostic belief and practice. Some of the Gnostic Gospels, especially *Thomas*, may even include valid historical remembrances of Jesus that are not found in the Bible.

Yet Christians believe that the biblical Gospels are unique, not only because they offer the most historically accurate portraits of Jesus but also because they are uniquely inspired by

God. This belief rests, to some extent, on the arguments of the early church leaders. It has to do with issues of age, usage, apostolicity, and orthodoxy. But Christian confidence in the Gospels goes beyond that which can be found in church history. It becomes a matter of faith as well as sight. In the next and final chapter I will reflect a bit further on trusting the Gospels and Christian faith.

Chapter 16

Can We Trust the Gospels After All?

As I explained in chapter 1, this book began as a series on my web site.[1] Thus it qualifies as a "blook," a book based on a blog.

There are advantages to writing a blook. One of the main ones is that, as an author, I can interact with my readers concerning the content of the book way before it is published. I can discover what works and what doesn't work, what persuades and what fails to convince. Before the final manuscript is submitted, I can revise and revamp, making what is ultimately published in book form better than it would have been in a "blogless" world. For this reason, as I was finishing my rewrite of the original series, I intentionally put up on my blog much of my new material.[2] This too has now been tested in the critical world of the blogosphere.

1. http://www.markdroberts.com/htmfiles/resources/gospelsreliable.htm.
2. http://www.markdroberts.com/htmfiles/resources/gospelsreliable-more.htm.

Positive Responses

Over the past year I've received hundreds of responses to the substance of this book from my blog readers. Most of these have been positive, otherwise I wouldn't have gone the blook route. A few of these favorable responses came at opportune moments. At one point I was struggling with a particularly difficult section, feeling discouraged that things were moving along so slowly, and wondering if it was all worth it. In the midst of my angst I received a sweet note from a young man who had been wracked with doubt about the Gospels. Through Google he found my blog series on the reliability of the Gospels, and it hit the intellectual spot. With his encouragement, I put my nose back to the grindstone and finished the tricky section.

Negative Responses

I have also received negative responses to my blog series on the Gospels. Most of these have been respectful, though a few have blended their criticisms with large doses of unkindness. I have taken the polite criticisms seriously, in some cases making corrections in my writing, in other cases strengthening my argument, and in still other cases simply acknowledging that people of good will can disagree about many things, including the Gospels.

I want to address directly some of the negative responses I've received because I expect this book will engender similar reactions. Moreover, responding to criticism will help me explain more clearly why I've written this book and what I hope to have accomplished.

Is the Book Unbalanced?

Some respondents to my blog series claimed that my scholarship was unbalanced. They accused me of weighting my arguments with academically conservative positions and overlooking material critical of the Gospels. Ironically, others were

188

uncomfortable with the extent to which I engaged critical scholarship, even accepting some critical conclusions.

I have tried to be as balanced as possible in my presentation of the data. Yes, I have used more conservative scholarship than you would find in some writers. And I've drawn more generously from the liberal side than other writers. I suppose that's what you get with someone who has my eclectic background.

But I do want to reiterate something from chapter 1. I have not based my argument for the reliability of the Gospels on the most conservative theories. Although I find some of these theories are enticing, I have intentionally stayed in the mainstream of New Testament scholarship. My point in doing so is to show that, even taking most of the facts as they're portrayed in the typical college religion course, you can still trust the Gospels. If more conservative theories turn out to be true, so much the better.

I have not always gone with the critical party line, however. As we saw in chapter 11, much of New Testament scholarship is based on an anti-supernaturalistic worldview. This is simply taken for granted in much of the secular academy and among scholars with liberal theology. But, as a result, many of the "assured results of scholarship" rest on an unreliable foundation, and I don't receive much assurance from them.

Is This Book Too Popular?

When I was studying at Harvard, Elaine Pagels, a graduate of the doctoral program there, had just published her best-selling book *The Gnostic Gospels*.[3] She was the talk of the town among New Testament faculty and students. Some of them applauded Pagels, both for her positive treatment of Gnosticism and for her ability to communicate academic theories to a wider audience. Many criticized Pagels, however, not for what she had written but for the fact that she was attempt-

3. Elaine Pagels, *The Gnostic Gospels* (New York: Random, 1979).

ing to write for a lay audience. "Real scholars," it was said, "write for scholars. Pagels is a *popularizer*." The tone of this critique suggested that a popularizer was little more than an academic sideshow act, somebody akin to a sword swallower in the circus.

I actually admire Elaine Pagels's ability to communicate with a wide audience. Though I'm not fond of many of her ideas, I must acknowledge that she is an effective communicator outside the hallowed halls of academia. A certain amount of popularizing is good. The word *popular* comes from the Latin term meaning "belonging to the people." A popularizer takes that which is hard for ordinary people to understand and makes it available to them. With this in mind, I'll confess to being a popularizer, one who seeks to translate the data of New Testament scholarship for those who aren't experts.

The challenge for the popularizer is remaining academically responsible. One of my criticisms of Pagels is that she conveniently overlooks scholarly data that doesn't fit her case. Over-simplification is always a danger for those who try to simplify the complex. I recognize this risk, and have attempted to overcome it.

I have been pleasantly surprised by positive comments on my blog series from experts in New Testament studies, including professors and pastors with advanced degrees in New Testament. I say "pleasantly surprised" because I've been well aware that every single chapter in this book could become a long, scholarly treatise. Yet my effort, by its very design, summarizes complex issues simply while neglecting arcane complications from which scholars make their careers. Therefore I'm glad that some experts can see the value in what I'm doing here and can appreciate it for what it is.

Is This Book Too Apologetic?

For some critics of Christianity, calling something apologetic is one of the worst insults of all. If a book is apologetic, then it is utterly suspect and unworthy of serious consideration. I'm sure some folks will quickly discover that my book is apologetic, and they'll send plenty of invective in my direction. I had one e-mailer tell me I was a "terrible philosopher" and a "dishonest liar" because of how I had defended the Gospels. I'm surprised he didn't accuse me of being an apologist!

Yes, this book is apologetic. Remember, this doesn't mean I'm apologizing for anything. Rather, apologetic writing seeks to defend and explain matters of faith. It takes on attacks against Christianity and tries to blunt them. Positively, apologists build a compelling case for Christian faith, one that registers not only with believers but also with unbelievers. The greatest of recent apologists, C. S. Lewis, was a master of this effort.

So, yes, this book is in the genre of apology. If you believe that any effort to defend the Christian faith is a waste of time, then you'd be better off not bothering with this book. (Of course it's highly unlikely that anyone who thinks thus will ever read this far, anyway!)

Ironically, some of those who have dismissed my writing as too apologetic have been Christians who, I think, believe that apologetics is unnecessary. These folks seem either to be academics who dislike popularization—something essential to most apologetic writing—or Christians who see the whole enterprise as unnecessary.

Is This Book Unnecessary?

I know many Christians who have a robust faith in the authority of Scripture. They easily laugh off the silliness of *The Da Vinci Code* or remain unperturbed when liberal scholars get lots of press for their denigrations of the Bible. Some of these hearty believers may respond to my book in this way: "Hey, it's all well and good that you believe the Gospels are reliable. But your arguments are unnecessary. The Gospels appear in the Bible, after all, God's inspired Word. If they're in Scripture, then surely they're trustworthy. What other evidence do you need?"

This is a valid theological defense of the Gospels. In fact, I believe the biblical evangelists were inspired by God. But defending the Gospels on the basis of their divine inspiration does not help the person who is uncertain about whether or not they are inspired. This argument doesn't work for the Christian who is doubting the inspiration of Scripture because of concerns about the historical reliability of the Gospels. And it surely doesn't work for the person who isn't a Christian and who wants to know if the biblical portraits of Jesus can stand on their own as historically accurate sources.

I have written this book primarily for people who have questions and doubts about the Gospels. Maybe these doubts have come in a natural process of intellectual growth. Maybe they stem from a college religion class . . . or a popular book by a scholar who disparages the Gospels . . . or an interview on NPR . . . or a newspaper article on the Jesus Seminar . . . or a *Newsweek* cover story that undermines confidence in the Gospels . . . or a popular novel that claims the most accurate portrayals of Jesus are to be found in the "unaltered" and "earlier" Gospels found outside of the Bible[4] . . . or you name it. Our world today abounds with challenges to the dependability of the Gospels. What was once limited to the academy has now pervaded popular culture and cannot be ignored.

I wish this book were unnecessary. I wish the Gospels weren't under assault in the academy and in pop culture. But wishful thinking won't change reality. I expect that, long after *The Da Vinci Code* has been forgotten and the Gospel of Judas is collecting dust in theological libraries, other attacks upon the Gospels will come. Thus there will be an ongoing need for a basic, readable, popular, apologetic explanation of their reliability. That's what I've tried to write.

Orthodox Christians believe that the Bible is God's Word. We also believe that the Bible is a human book, written by human beings over the course of many centuries. Keeping the two natures of the Bible together isn't easy. Even as Christians

---

4. Dan Brown, *The Da Vinci Code* (New York: Doubleday, 2003), 248, 234.

throughout the ages have struggled to keep the humanity and the deity of Christ together, so we struggle when it comes to Scripture. In this book I have focused on the human dimension of the Gospels because it is important. Yet nothing I've said about the Gospels denies their divine inspiration.

Can We Trust the Gospels?

I began this book with a simple question: *Can we trust the Gospels?* I explained that I was thinking in terms of two different but related questions. The first had to do with history: Can we trust the Gospels to provide reliable historical information about Jesus of Nazareth? The second was a matter of faith: Do the Gospels offer a trustworthy basis for faith in Jesus?

I've spent the bulk of this book answering the first question. I've tried to show that we can indeed trust the Gospels when it comes to the question of history. I do not believe, however, that I've *proven* beyond any doubt that the New Testament Gospels are historically reliable. Historical arguments about the 2,000-year-old past, it seems to me, are too complex and convoluted for verdicts declared with a ring of certainty.

Ironically, these days it's often the skeptical scholars who seem to have cornered the market on certainty. And as long as they write mainly for each other, talk mainly to each other, and make sure their scholarly publications and meetings are dominated by each other's work, these skeptical scholars can pretend as if their "assured results of scholarship" are rock solid. In fact, however, they're often more like a house of cards built on the sand, if you'll pardon an intentionally mixed metaphor.

I don't object to scholars holding views that doubt or even deny the reliability of the Gospels. But I do object to scholars holding these views without ever taking seriously the evidence that would challenge or contradict them. This seems not only disingenuous but also bad scholarship.[5] Sometimes conservative scholars too quickly disregard the insights of critical scholars. For the most part, however, conservative scholars must deal with a broad range of scholarly input, while skeptical scholars can remain safely protected within their conveniently narrow worlds.

I mentioned above that I don't believe I've proved beyond a reasonable doubt that the New Testament Gospels are historically reliable. I do believe, however, that I've shown it is reasonable to trust the Gospels as historically accurate. Though certain elements of the Gospels are problematic in this regard, I find that the evidence, when taken as a whole, strongly supports the view that the biblical Gospels paint a reliable picture of Jesus (or, to be more precise, several accurate, complementary pictures of Jesus).

If your worldview excludes the possibility of miracles, then you have an intractable problem with the historicity of the Gospels. But your acceptance of such a worldview is a matter of faith. There's no way you can prove that miracles don't happen, even as there's no way I can prove that they do. There's an irreducible element of faith on both sides of this argument.

Nevertheless, my point is that one can approach the New Testament Gospels as a theist and come up with a reasonable understanding of what actually happened, of who Jesus was and how early Christianity developed. Of course I believe that this understanding is not only reasonable but in fact is the most reasonable. Yet I'm willing to debate the pros and cons with those who disagree with me. What I'm unwilling to do is to accept the tyranny of "the modern scientific worldview" or to agree that historians must write as if miracles never happen.

5. There are some skeptical scholars on Jesus who do take seriously more conservative work. One of the things I like about Marcus Borg, perhaps the most prolific and popularly influential fellow of the Jesus Seminar, is his willingness to engage in serious dialogue with N. T. Wright, a critical scholar who has come to many conservative conclusions about Jesus. See the book they have written together: Marcus Borg and N. T. Wright, *The Meaning of Jesus: Two Visions* (San Francisco: HarperSanFrancisco, 2000).

I'm happy to take my theistic understanding of the Gospels and lay it beside all other options for careful scrutiny. At the very least, a fair observer would have to acknowledge that what I've proposed is reasonable, even if that observer doesn't buy it.

Throughout most of these chapters I've spoken of the Gospels as reliable, meaning "reliable as historical sources of information about Jesus." Yet I believe, now speaking as a Christian more than as a historian, that the Gospels are much more reliable than this. Aside from being trustworthy history, the Gospels are also trustworthy revelation. I believe that the very Spirit of God inspired and guided the writers of the Gospels. This means the portrayal of Jesus in Mark, for example, isn't only historically reliable. It's also God's way of helping us know who Jesus really is.

What I'm saying here goes beyond historical inquiry. Yet I want to emphasize that what I have found as a historian doesn't imply that my faith in the inspiration of the Gospels is really just wishful thinking. On the contrary, the more I study the New Testament Gospels in the context of the literature and culture of their own time and place, and the more I compare these biblical Gospels to the noncanonical varieties, the more I am persuaded that Matthew, Mark, Luke, and John are indeed reliable both as historical records of Jesus and as trustworthy facets of divine revelation.

Can we trust the Gospels? In a word, *yes.*

General Index

Scripture Index

202